A Garland Series

The English Stage

Attack and Defense 1577 - 1730

A collection of 90 important works
reprinted in photo-facsimile in 50 volumes

edited by
Arthur Freeman
Boston University

Collier Tracts
1698

with a preface
for the Garland Edition by

Arthur Freeman

Garland Publishing, Inc., New York & London

1974

Library of Congress Cataloging in Publication Data
Main entry under title:

Collier tracts, 1698.

Reprint of the 1698 editions of The immorality of the English pulpit (anonymous), printed in London; of A letter to A. H. Esq., concerning the stage (attributed to Charles Hopkins), printed for A. Baldwin, London; of A letter to Mr. Congreve on his pretended amendments (anonymous), printed for S. Keble, London; of Some remarks upon Mr. Collier's defence of his short view of the English stage (anonymous), printed for A. Baldwin, London; of The occasional paper: number IX, containing some considerations about the danger of going to plays, by Richard Willis, Bishop of Winchester, printed for M. Wotton, London; and of A vindication of the stage (anonymous), printed for J. Wild, London.

1. Theater--Moral and religious aspects. 2. Theater--England--History--Sources.
PN2047.C68 1974 792'.013 76-170453
ISBN 0-8240-0610-0

Printed in the United States of America

Contents

Preface

This volume contains six short contributions to the original "Collier controversy," all of 1698. The Immorality of the English Pulpit *is a squib dedicated to the disapprobation of Collier by an ironic application of his arguments to preaching, but its own weakness and facetiousness leave it, in its brevity, a rhetorical failure. We reprint it (Lowe-Arnott-Robinson 313, Hooker 18) from a copy in the British Museum (116.b.47), collating* A^4.

A Letter to A. H. *is attributed questionably by Lowe-Arnott-Robinson to Charles Hopkins, following Sister Rose Anthony, but is relegated to anonymity by Hooker (9). Wing unaccountably gives it to Luke Milbourne; an edition with apparatus is provided by H. T. Swedenberg, Jr.,* Essays on the Stage *[Augustan Reprint Society] (1946). The addressee may be Anthony Hammond or Anthony Horneck. Wing M 2033, advertised June 11-13, 1698; Lowe-Arnott-Robinson 314. We reprint the British Museum copy (011795.h.2), collating* A^1 B-C^4 D^2 E^1 *(=A2?).*

A Letter to Mr. Congreve *is discussed, as are many of the included pamphlets, by D. Crane Taylor,* William Congreve *(Oxford, 1931), as well as by Sister Rose Anthony and J. W. Krutch. It was advertised in the* Post Man *for 30 August-September 1, as to be published "tomorrow," and we reprint the British Museum copy (641.b.37[1]), collating* A-E^4 F^3. *Wing L 1713a, Lowe-Arnott-Robinson 315, Hooker 14. In the same vein is* Some Remarks upon Mr. Collier's Defence. *We reprint the British Museum copy (641.b.37[2]), with the half title supplied from a copy at the University of Cincinnati; the collation is* A-B^4 C^3. *Wing S 4605; Lowe-Arnott-Robinson 320.*

The Occasional Paper: Number IX. Containing some Considerations about the Danger of Going to Plays *is probably by Richard Willis, Bishop of Winchester, as the edition by H. T. Swedenberg, Jr., indicates (*Essays on the Stage, *1946), although* DNB *remains aloof. We reprint the original edition of 1698, evidently not in Wing (Lowe-Arnott-Robinson 316, Hooker 5, advertised 19-21 May), from the British Museum copy (4378.cc.34), collating* A-F^2.

A Vindication of the Stage *has been attributed, tentatively and improbably, by J. W. Krutch to Charles Gildon, but remains traditionally anonymous. It was advertised on 17-19 May; Wing V 532, Lowe-Arnott-Robinson 323, Hooker 4. We reprint the British Museum copy (641.e.52), collating* A-C^4 D^3.

May, 1973 A. F.

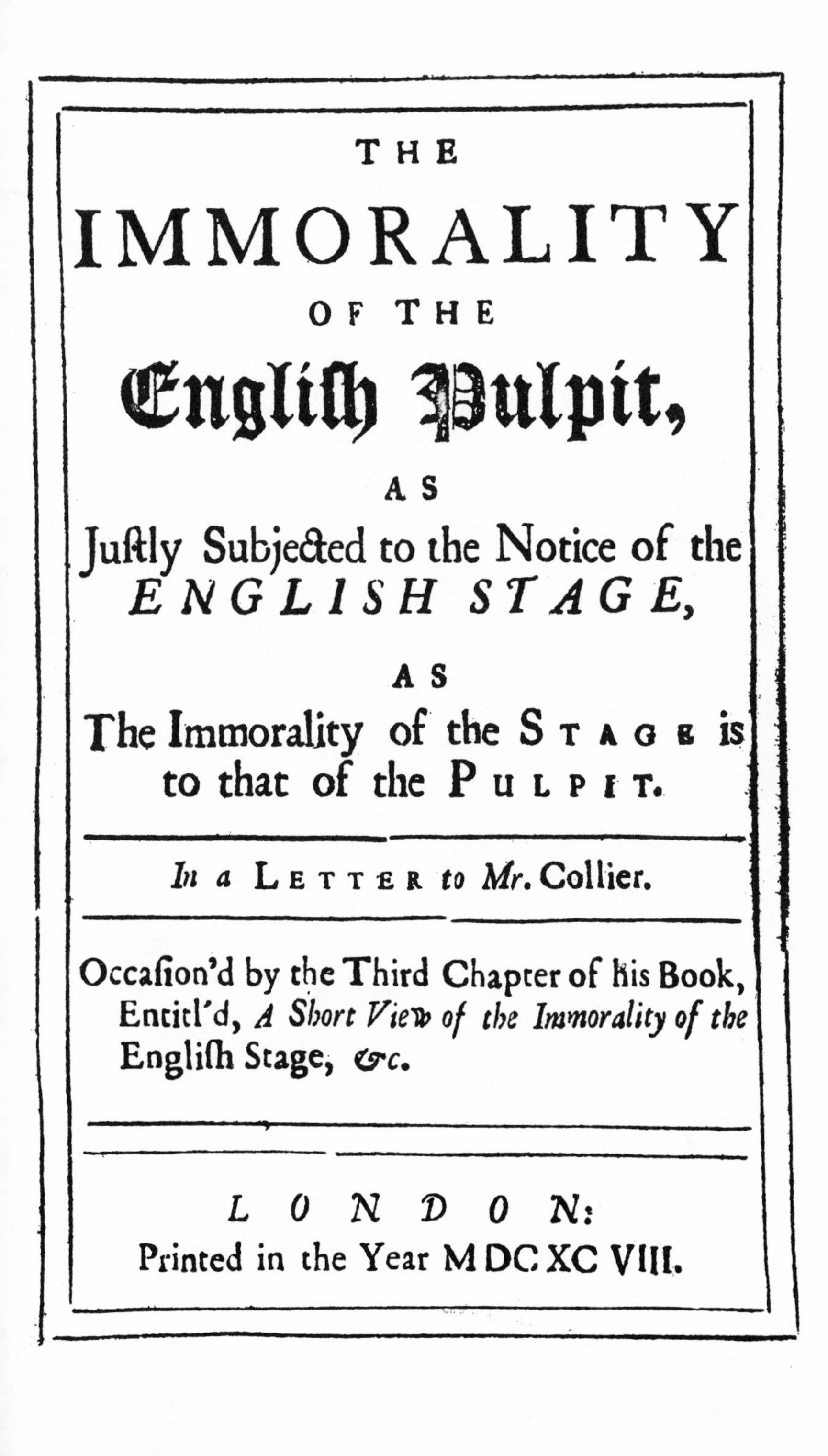

THE

IMMORALITY

OF THE

English Pulpit,

AS

Justly Subjected to the Notice of the *ENGLISH STAGE*,

AS

The Immorality of the STAGE is to that of the PULPIT.

In a LETTER *to Mr.* Collier.

Occasion'd by the Third Chapter of his Book, Entitl'd, *A Short View of the Immorality of the* English Stage, *&c.*

LONDON:
Printed in the Year MDCXCVIII.

A Word to Mr. *Collier*, by way of EPISTLE, concerning his Short-(sighted)-View of *the Immoralities of the* English *Stage*, &c.

SIR,

THAT the Licentiousness of the Stage should ask the Correction of your Pen, is a sad and manifold Confession of the Degeneracy of the Times, and withal shews the pressingness of the Occasion. What else could provoke a man to write against himself? For 'tis to your dear Times that we owe the vileness of the Theatre; Those very Loose Times, to the Protector whereof you are so constant a Devotee; so that in the Cause depending you are both Plaintiff and Defendant. And though you may chance to win the Saddle, yet you can't but lose the Horse *and go within a hair's-breadth of making an* Ass *of your self.*

THAT a Parson (Cashier'd for Misbehaviour) should devote his Idleness to the Reading of Plays is no strange Matter; but that such an one should snarl over his beloved Diet, is remarkably Currish; however not at all beside his Character. But though he lets us understand he has still the same Faculties about him; yet he wisely informs us at the same time that he has alter'd his Object, and left off his fruitless Barking at the *Moon above* him, for the sake of a *Cynthia*, that may be brought *under*. And indeed he has wrestled notably with the bright Dame of the Stage; whom that he might enjoy more safely, he endeavours to strip naked of Applause, and so preserve her from being Clapt by any one but himself. A notable piece of Christianity, and becoming the Piety and Policy of the Party! *But the Stage is Corrupted, ill Humours are Predominant, and something must be Administred to curb these Excesses.* Very good; but must a Parson needs step out of the huge Throng of Quacks, clap on the Spectacles, and apply the Glister-pipe, purely to discover his Knowledge in *Fundamentals*? No, no, there is something more in it than all this comes to, or else the Stage might e'en have perish'd or prosper'd under its *Immodesty*, *Prophaneness*, *Immorality*, &c.

for

for him: And a Thousand *Sebastians*, *King Arthurs*, *Donquixots*, and *Relapses* might have Club'd their Impudence to Hoot Virtue out of the World, had they but deported themselves as they should have done to a man in his Garb; then should they never have been confronted with, and brought to receive Sentence from the Ancient *Pagans*, the *State*, or the *Church*. Nor had all those *Hydra* Heads mention'd in his *Contents* ever been discover'd or brought to the Correction of his *Chopping-knife*.

But they are rightly served, they must be peeping, forsooth, into the Pleats of the *Gown*, and presume to look Vermin upon Sacred *Cloth*; ay, and to search for Petticoats under the Cassock. Now, wou'd any Parson alive, think ye, have patience to endure this Operation, and not rather have a Louse graze all its life upon his Gleab, than to undergo the pinch of having it knack'd, which causes more pains than a Twelvemonth's biting? But you'll say it is foolish on both sides to quarrel about a March of Louse-hunting, especially considering how fatal the Consequences may be to both; for Mr. *Ray* has an old Proverb (but of daily use) that *when some sort of folks fall out, a better sort may chance to hear of their own again.* So that, in my opinion, they had better a draw'd back their stakes before

fore it had come to this ; for to have the Artillery of the Church drawn out in Order of Battle, charged with Anathema's and Excommunications; ramm'd down with the Papers of Ancient Writers, and Modern Rehearsers; primed with combustible Ambition, and then fired-with red hot Passion, must needs make a confounded Clatter against the Deal-boards of a Stage, and give the Alarm to the *Honest World to shift for it self*, and then those two topping Vocations would be worse than *Silk-weaving*.

Tis to be confess'd, the Stage is grown as Corrupt and Immoral, as the Pulpit can be for the Life on't ; and I see no reason why Mr. *Collier* may not, if he pleases, return them a *Rowland* for their *Oliver* ; I frankly agree, that most of his Charge against them is just, undeniable, and well seconded with Proofs. But I must beg his pardon, if it be an Affront to tell him, that his Hat hung in his Light when he wrote that *Chapter*, wherein he accuses the Stage as *guilty of abusing the Clergy*. For he has not been so kind as to shew one Instance wherein they are abused, but on the contrary, has cited several Historical Passages, Translated by the Poets indeed into Verse, but taken Originally from the Works of his own Party, as may too easily be made ap-

pear ;

pear; nay, I durſt engage my ſelf to accommodate every accuſed Paſſage with a warrantable Text. Now, certainly if the Stage has any buſineſs in the World, it is to ridicule Vice with all the Powers of Wit, to expoſe the chief Patrons of it; to lay open the Hypocrite to the common View of the World, and to dawb his outſide of the ſame Colour as within. It is the Office of the Stage to detect the *Roguery*, as well as the *Folly* of a *Knave*; and if ſuch a one creeps into the Pulpit, 'tis their Concern to cry *Ware ſhins* to the gaping Auditory, leſt whilſt he is drawing their Eyes towards the Pulpit-Roof, he ſhould let them unawares through a Trap-door into Hell. A wicked Parſon is the moſt potent Villain upon Earth; he not only abuſes a *Man*, but a *World*, and endeavours to put the Cheat upon God himſelf. Whilſt he chews the Goſpel in his Mouth, he infects it, and makes a deadly Poyſon of the *Bread of Life*, which he ſpits out upon the Congregation, becauſe it agrees not with his own Palate. And yet Roguery of this fatal kind is not extenſive nor general enough, in Mr. *Collier's* opinion, to be taken notice of by the Stage. But I wou'd fain know what an Univerſal Rogue is, if this ben't his Character? A *Lay*-Raſcal has no ſuch Capacity, he contents himſelf with ſome peculiar in the *Practick*, as the

Cutting a Purse, the Tricking a Client, the Killing a Patient, or, to go one degree further, the Buying at a great Rate a Copy of some Master in the Faculty, whereby the Author is encouraged to prosecute his Studies, and the Bookseller obliged for Interest sake to make him as many Proselytes as he can. This is indeed the perfection of Mechanick Roguery, and Knave and Fool well mixt. But, alas! these know nothing of the Theory, are not acquainted with the Sublimities of Vice, have not that advantageous View of the whole System, as those from the Pulpit have. And is the Stage blameable for making it their Business (upon all occasions) to unriddle the Mystery of Iniquity, and to Counter-plot them? Or is it more Criminal in the Stage to *Act* that in a *Play* which they *do* in *Earnest*? Or why should not that *Parson* make up a Character in a Comedy, and be personated by a *Player*, who personates a *Player* in the *Pulpit*, and interlopes upon the Stage, by turning the *Church* into a *Play-house*? Certainly it is but just Retaliation; and that Parson (tho' it were Mr. *Collier*) who appropriates the Lashes of the Stage to himself, or is offended at the Stage in this particular, is either an Abetter or a Partaker of the Vices of the Clergy, and so most justly subjected to the Notice of the *English Stage*.

FINIS.

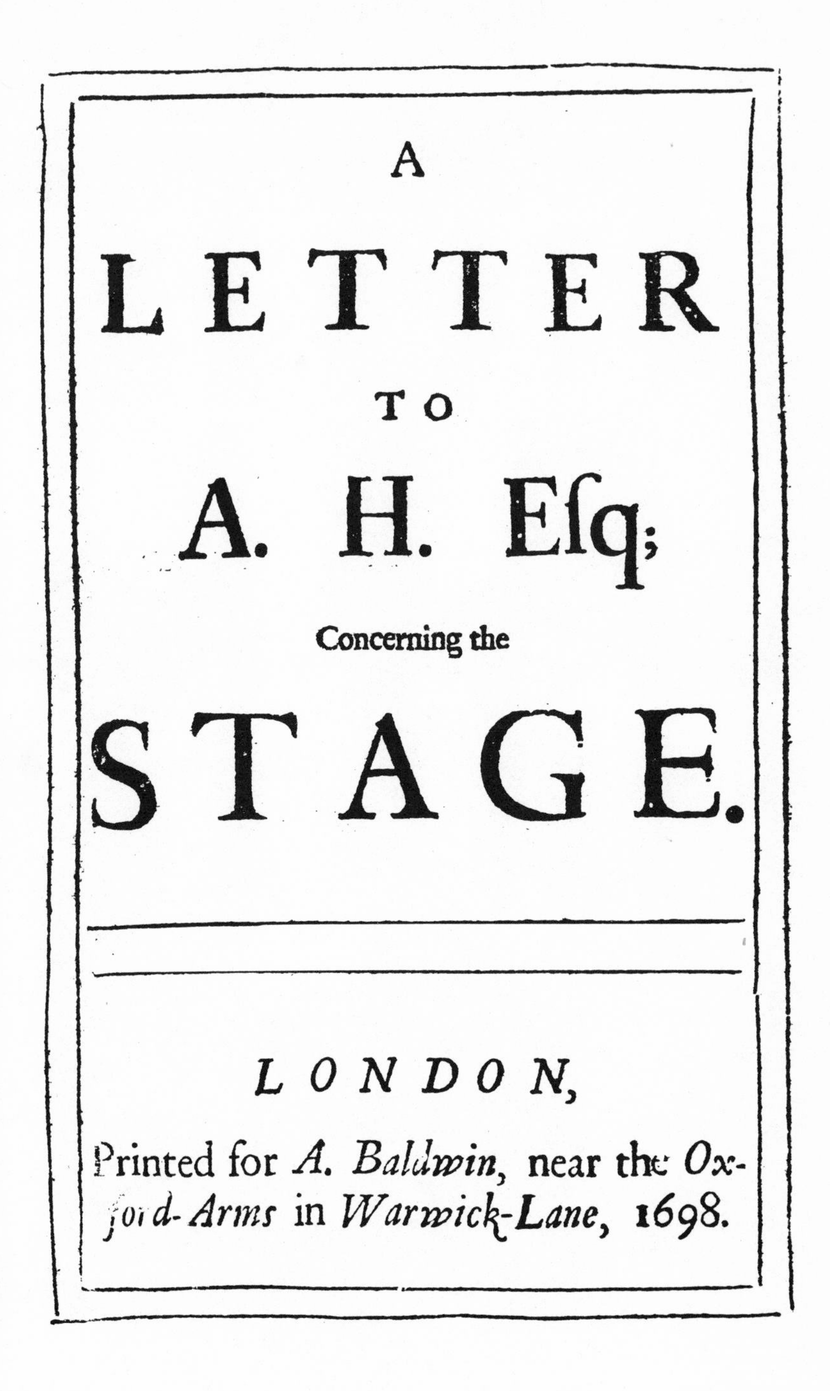

A

LETTER

TO

A. H. Esq;

Concerning the

STAGE.

LONDON,

Printed for *A. Baldwin*, near the *Ox-ford-Arms* in *Warwick-Lane*, 1698.

TO
A. H. Esq; *&c.*

SIR,

FOrgive me if I think it Ill-nature in you to leave the Town, at a Time when it wants your Company, and seems to beg your Assistance: How can you propose to live at Ease in the Country, when so many of your Friends, the Wits, are engag'd here in open War? Let Mr. *Collier* say what he pleases of Mr. *Dryden*, I begin to think 'twas his prophetick Genius mov'd him to declaim against Priests; and there is great reason to complain of their being the Incendiaries of the People, when they set the World on fire by Preaching, which they were only sent to warm. But what can Mr. *Collier* mean by exposing the Stage so? he wou'd not surely have it silenc'd: That wou'd be a little too barbarous, and too much like Cant to be entertain'd by Men of Thought or Ingenuity. I wou'd rather suppose he design'd a Reformation; and that is so reasonable, I wonder any Man should put his Face in disorder, or study a Revenge for the Attempt. But it may be ask'd, Cou'd he not have done that without exposing so many great *Genius's*? Had it not been better to have let Mr. *Durfey* alone? Tho' even this Method wou'd not have pleas'd every body; for whate'er Effect it has had on Mr. *Vanbroug* and *Congreve*; *Motteux* and *Guildon* resent it to the last degree. Is their nothing in their Works Illustrious, or that cou'd merit Censure? Indeed some People are not to be reclaim'd by Ridicule; and Mr. *Collier* knowing their Vertues, with how much Compos'dness and Resignation they can bear a Hiss, out of Compassion, took Example by the Town and neglected both.

It is the Observation of some, That wherever the State flourishes, the Theatre has never fail'd of Encouragement; and that 'tis hardly possible the State shou'd suffer without the others sinking in its Reputation. It is Pity that *England* shou'd be the only Exception, and since we have some of our Nobility, who have a Taste of Eloquence, and all those Vertues which adorn the Stage, that It shou'd want their Assistance by whom it was at first rais'd, and since maintain'd: If it has fallen from its Purity, or never arriv'd to what they fully lik'd, let it not want their Countenance, without whom 'tis impossible to be any thing at all, and by whom it may become all that we can wish. They alone can free it from Contempt and Censure, by maintaining such an Awe, that the least Glymps of Profaneness and Immorality shou'd not dare to appear on the

the Stage; and this may be done by encouraging none but those who write well: for when a good Poet takes on him to instruct, we need fear no Immodesty; for 'tis impossible in a Regular Play, he shou'd find room for an Indecency. I know you'll ask, Why shou'd I appear so zealous in desiring the Favour of the Nobility for what is deny'd to be lawful; and that I ought not to wish an Encouragement of the Stage, when 'tis affirm'd that from Thence we derive our Corruption of Manners. Mr. *Collier* has endeavour'd to prove this from the Looseness of some of our Plays, and then has brought the Opinion of the Fathers to condemn the Theatre in general.

As to the *First* Objection, *That the Debauchery of the Town is to be attributed to the Looseness of our Plays and Stage.*

If this were true, it is an Objection only against the present Corruption of the Theatre; and is of no force against a regulated Stage; for that admits of nothing Immodest or Immoral.

As to the *Second* Objection brought from Councils and Fathers, if what is quoted were really design'd by them against the Theatre in general, yet it can have but little effect with the People, I mean the Men of Probity and Learning; for they are not to be mov'd by the Opinions of others no longer than those Opinions are agreeable to Reason: No Man ought to pay such a Respect either to Councils or Fathers, as to submit his Judgment

 con-

contrary to his Reaſon. Their ſaying ſo in this Caſe ought to have no more effect with us than if they had at the ſame time given us their Opinion of the Truth of *Tranſubſtantiation*.

I think the Matter ought to be diſputed by it ſelf; for the Opinion of the Fathers cannot alter the Nature of the Thing. Sir, give me leave to make this Digreſſion: 'Tis my Opinion, even in Matters of Religion, the preaching up the Fathers ſo much has been of fatal Conſequence. If we run out of our ſelves to ſearch for Truth, we are expos'd to be deceiv'd; and relying too much upon another's Judgment, may be the occaſion of an Errour in our own. A falſe Quotation or Interpretation by a Man of ſome Figure, to an eaſie Credulous Bigot, has been the Converſion of a great many, and of excellent Service in the Church of *Rome*: They cannot attack any without a Father or Council, and that to a Perſon who knows nothing of the matter, is as good as a Demonſtration. The Fathers were but Men, and as capable to be deceiv'd as others: And I do not know why the Biſhop of *Worceſter* may not deſerve an equal Eſteem; he underſtands the Languages, and has as much Sincerity as any of them; and why then ſhou'd he not be able to give the Senſe of the Scripture as well.

I have a Veneration for them as good Men, and where their Opinion is a Conſequent of true Reaſon, it ought to be embraced; but where 'tis

not

not, I need not ſay it ought to be rejected; and I think any Man may be allowed to diſpute whether it be ſo or no. The Biſhop of *Worceſter* cannot publiſh a Book, but you'll have an Anſwer to it. It would indeed be of Reputation to the Councils and Fathers, ſome of them at leaſt, if what were objected againſt them were of no more force. His Philoſophy is too rational to be weak'ned by Sophiſtry; his Divinity too ſolid to be ſhook by Hereſie: He ſeems to have been predeſtinated to Glory, and the appointed Inſtrument to deliver us from Popery, Atheiſm, Deiſm, and Socinianiſm, with all thoſe ſpurious Sectaries which have been ſpawned into the World: What can reſiſt the Power of his Arguments? And who is able to abide his Force. But to return, I think the Controverſie, in ſhort, is this:

Whether the Allowance of a Theatre in a Chriſtian Country, is conſiſting with the Chriſtian Religion.

The Anſwer to this Queſtion may be this:

That whatever is approved by lawful Authority, and is not againſt any poſitive revealed Law of God, is conſiſting with the Chriſtian Religion.

Now it lies upon the Adverſaries of the Stage to prove, That the Theatre is againſt Law or Scripture.

'Tis

'Tis unfair to take the advantage of the present Corruptions, and cry down the Stage, because Men make an ill use of it. The Priests won't allow this Argument in another Case; and I think an ill Poet is no more an Objection against the Stage, than a Clergyman's being a Blockhead, is to the Pulpit. 'Tis our Misfortune to have too many in both Vocations; tho, as bad as the Stage is, I don't doubt but the World has receiv'd a great many Advantages from it. I shall name you some, and the first may be the reclaiming the Manners of the Clergy.

Tis certain, since the Stage has used the Gown freely, and the Laity have not been afraid to look into their Faults, that they are more humble, and less publickly vicious: They know if *Tom D'urfey* can light upon a frail Priest, he won't scruple to expose his Infirmities, tho' he is not the only *Whipping Tom* of the Stage; if they had not others to fear, they wou'd soon grow too many for him. I believe they wou'd be angry, if they thought the People gave the Honour of their Reformation to the Stage; tho' you can't believe otherwise, if you consider the difference of the former and present Clergy, what a strange alteration there is where the Knowledge of Plays have come (I wou'd be understood only of those who needed a Reformation) There are now, and have always been, Men among them able and fit to give Laws, and from whom the World was glad to receive them, who appear'd as burning

ing and ſhining Lights in their Generation; and it was from them we learnt the difference; it was their Light which expos'd the other, and the Stage only took their evil Deeds, to ſhew them truly the Evils of them. But beſides their Reforming of Manners, the Stage has taught them to ſpeak Engliſh, and preach more like Ambaſſadors of their great Maſter. It has taught them to argue rationally, and at once mended their Stile, and Form of their Sermons. How did Religion labour under heavy Language, and how many People rather abſented the Church, than come to hear the Word of God Burleſqu'd? In what a ridiculous Dreſs did Religion appear? When to ſpin out the time in old Proverbs, and wretched Puns, a Fellow wou'd run it up to *Six and thirtiethly*, before he came to his *Uſe* and *Applications*. In ſhort, the Drunkenneſs, Whoring, Inſolence, and Dulneſs that has appear'd under a Black Coat on the Stage, have made the Men of the ſame Colour of it keep within Bounds: And that a Man might not teize them with the Repreſentation, they have endeavour'd to appear in as differing a Form as poſſible.

If what Mr. *Collier* ſays was true, That when a Clergyman is brought on the Stage, it is with a deſign to ridicule the Function, it wou'd be abominable, and as bad as the Town is, wou'd be hiſs'd off the Stage. I dare ſay, whatever the Intention of the Poet is, 'tis not receiv'd ſo by the Audience. For at this rate, every fooliſh Peer who is brought on the Stage, muſt be be ſuppoſ'd to intend a Reflection on all the Men of Condition; and an Alderman, who is a Cuckold, muſt be look'd on as the Repreſentative of his Brethren. 'Tis abſurd to make no diſtinction; as if a particular Vice in a particular Man, cou'd not be expos'd without a deſign'd Reflection on all who belong to him. It ought to touch no body but whom it concerns; and it has its end, if it reclaims where it was deſign'd, and prevents others, by ſhewing the Danger: And this is the Deſign of Comedy. But the Queſtion is, Whether our Poets have managed it as they ought? Whether they have not pick'd out a particular Perſon, and expos'd the Character in general, under the Notion of one Man? I anſwer to this, That whatever the Deſign of the Poet has been, it has not had the effect with the People: For who disbelieves the Authority of their Function, or thinks the worſe of Good, Learned, and Ingenious Men among them? Are not the Religious very much reverenc'd? Has any Body thought the worſe of *Stillingfleet*, *Tillotſon*, and *Burnet*, upon this Account? Who can believe, that when Mr. *Vanbroug* diſguiſes a Parſon, that he thought of theſe Men, or any who lives ſoberly, and makes Religion their Buſineſs, and at the ſame time, don't make it inconſiſtent with good Manners? The Good among them know the People love them, and that nothing but their own miſ-behaviour draws them into Contempt. Any Miniſter, tho' he was but of mean Underſtanding, yet if he had other good Qualities, if he liv'd

ſoberly

ſoberly, and did his Duty religiouſly, that ever ſuch a Man was pickt out to be the Scandal of his Neighbours, or a Ridicule of the Stage. Whence is it then, that the Clergy are ſo angry? If you hook but one of them, all the reſt are upon your Back, and you can't expoſe his Vices without being an Enemy to the Church: And in this, *Prieſts of all Religions are the ſame.*

But after all, why ſhou'd Mr. *Collier* blame Mr. *Dryden* for making *Dorax* exclaim againſt the *Mahometan* Prieſt? Or how can that be a Prejudice to the Character of the Chriſtian Clergy? Is it not natural for ſuch a one as *Dorax* to ſay as much, and eſpecially againſt ſuch a one as the *Mufti* in the Play? And does Mr. *Collier* blame Mr. *Dryden* for writing naturally? I think it is a Fault throughout Mr. *Collier*'s Book, that in his Criticiſms of the Plays, he never conſiders the Perſon who ſpeaks; that is, Whether 'tis not natural for a Man of ſuch a Character, to ſay ſuch a thing? It wou'd have been of more Service to have proved, That no Perſon is to be brought on the Stage to ſay an ill thing, and then he had thrown away all the Profaneneſs, which is ſo much an Offence, at once. But if ſuch Perſons are to be repreſented, there is not ſo much Reaſon againſt any of our preſent Plays, as is urg'd by Mr. *Collier*; for you muſt allow a Coquett to talk like her ſelf, a Lover to vent his Paſſion in Raptures, and a Rake to ſpeak the Language of the Town.

I have already told you, That I am far from vindicating the preſent Stage. I don't know a regular Play, or that ought to be repreſented on a regular Stage; yet I know a great many Plays that I would not looſe for want of that Regularity. Who wou'd not have Sir *G. Etheridge*, Mr. *Wicherly*, and even ſome of Mr. *Dryden*'s Plays? Who would reject the *Orphan*, becauſe Mr. *Collier* objects againſt a looſe Speech in it.

But Mr. *Collier* has laid other things to the Poet's Charge beſides the Abuſe of the Clergy; and that the profane Characters in the Play, has had an ill Effect on the Age, by promoting of Immorality and Vice. This I very much queſtion; for I can't apprehend ſo much danger even in the preſent Stage as Mr. *Collier* wou'd ſuggeſt. The greateſt Faults of our Plays are their being generally, in one part or other, unnatural: That which is regular in any of them can never be an Offence; and where that Monſter appears, it rather frightens than allures; ſo that we are not in ſo much danger, even from our very bad Plays: For the more monſtrous, the leſs Power it has to pleaſe; and whatever looſes the Power, can never do much damage. So that if Mr. *Collier* ſhould make a Collection of *D'urfey*'s Works, who is there that wou'd become a Convert? And who wou'd turn Parſon to be drunk and beat the Watch? Or who wou'd be proud of an Imitation of any of his Heroes? Has any Body brought themſelves under his Character, in hopes to recommend

mend them to the World? It would be happy if the World had learnt no more Irreligion from the Pulpit than it has from the Stage; at least, the Consequence of the first has been more fatal. What dismal Effect has the holy Cant had upon the Multitude: What Rebellion, Blood-shed and Mischief have been encourag'd under the Name of *Sanctity*, *Religion*, and the *Good old Cause*. Whoever learnt to cut a King's Throat by seeing of Plays? But by going to Church, the People were instructed to *bind the King in Chains, and his Nobles in Fetters of Iron, That the Kingdom ought to be taken away, and given to the Saints*; And who wou'd not be a Saint for such an Inheritance? Who cou'd refuse resisting of Authority, when instead of *Damnation*, it was *coming forth to the Help of the Lord against the Mighty*? But this is but one Mischief of the Pulpit; this is only putting a Kingdom in Civil Broils, intestine Wars, and unnatural Murthers. But when Men of debauch'd Principles shall become the Teachers of the Nation, what may we not expect from their Industry and Sedition.

After all, my Lord *Foppington* was never design'd to teach People to speak or act like him; nor was it intended that the Ladies shou'd be byass'd by the Example of *Berinthia* to turn Coquetts. These and the like Characters in other Plays, are not propos'd as a Direction for the *Gallant Man*, or the *Vertuous Lady*; but that seeing how such Persons behave themselves on the Stage, that they may not make the like Figure in the World: but if any body ſhou'd rather be in love than terrified by theſe Examples, 'tis their Fault, and not the Poets, ſince the beſt things are liable to Corruptions. But it may be objected, That our Poets don't make Perſons ſpeak like themſelves. That indeed is a Fault, and I can't ſay any thing to excuſe it but this; That they who have the Judgment to know when a Poet ſpeaks improperly, ought to have ſo much Judgment, as not to be byaſſed by his Irregularities: The People who don't underſtand it, generally ſuppoſe, that what is Vertuous is to be imitated, and what is Vicious is to be avoided. That this is the general Obſervation of thoſe who frequent Plays, may juſtly be inferr'd from the Practice of the Town: For I challenge any Man to prove, That any one Vice, now in being, took its Riſe from the Stage. The Stage takes Examples from the Town. The Scene muſt be really acted in the World before it comes to be expos'd: So that whatever appears Vicious or Ridiculous, is owing to the Wickedneſs of the Times, and not to the Theatre. It may be objected, That what is generally acted on the Stage, if it was done before, yet it was done in private; but the Stage publiſhes it. To this I anſwer, That it does not intend to licenſe it, only to ſet it in a true Light, that it may be expos'd and ſhunn'd.

As to thoſe Objections, That the Actors are generally debauch'd, and of leud Converſation; and that no Perſon who is a known

Adulterer,

Adulterer, or Profane, ought to be encouraged: That the Play-house is a Resort of vicious Persons, and gives Opportunity to such who have wicked Inclinations. All these wou'd fall upon the advancement of a regular Stage; but as 'tis, the Objections are not levell'd Right; for the State is chargeable with the Immoralities. There are Laws for the Punishment of Vice; and if the Magistrate neglect his Duty, he must answer for it. I don't know that any body is oblig'd to a Conversation with the Players; and their Lives can influence only their Associates; and such they wou'd find, whether they are Players or not. When they are on the Stage they are confin'd to the Poets Language: And if we shou'd see Mr. *Powel* acting a Brave, Generous and Honest Part; or Mrs. *Knight*, a very Modest and Chaste one, it ought not to give us Offence; because we are not to consider what they are off the Stage, but whom they represent: We are to do by them as in Religion we do by the Priest, mind what they say, and not what they do. Tho' the Stage is not so abandon'd but that there are some Honest and Vertuous, for any thing the Town can say to the contrary. And I wou'd leave it to themselves, whether they don't find their Account in it; whether the Town is not more favourable on any Occasion; so that it ought to be an Encouragement to persist in their Vertue.

The Objection against the Play-House it self, because it gives Opportunities for Wickedness, is so trifling, it is hardly worth answering; for they

they who are vicioully inclin'd will find an Opportunity; and as long as the Toleration-Act is in force, there is never a Meeting in Town but will afford extraordinary Hints of that kind; the Morning and Evening Lectures are precious Seasons; Mr. *Doolittle* may thresh his Heart out, there will be Tares among the Wheat; and those Houses are haunted with a sort of Spirits that are not to be cast out with Prayer and Fasting.

I think from the little I have said, it is certain the Town has not been debauch'd by the Stage, and that 'tis much easier to demonstrate the Good, than prove the Evil Effect even of our bad Plays. I have shew'd that there has been a Vertue in them; and we might very well pardon them if it were only for that one Benefit, of being so serviceable to the reclaiming of the Clergy. If they can give me an Instance of any Play whose Vices have had so ill Effect with the People as to counter-balance the Good it has wrought in them, I shou'd set my self against the Stage too; but then as to other Advantages which we have receiv'd from the Plays of the first Rank, we are certainly very much in debt to them. The Refinement of our Tongue is principally owing to them; Good Manners and good Conversation is owing to our Comedy; and I don't doubt but some of our Tragedies have fired some with a Greatness of Spirit, and taught to act the Hero with Prudence, Vertue and Courage.

I shall conclude this part of my Letter with this Observation, that if the present Stage has not

not been so terrible an Enemy to Christianity, but on the contrary, has afforded a great deal of good to the World; that a Regulated Stage wou'd be of infinite Service to the Nation.

I have proposed it as an Argument in Defence of a Regular Stage, that it lies on its Adversaries to prove it against Law or Scripture, and so might leave it justify'd till some Person or other make the Discovery to the World: But because 'tis my Opinion 'tis utterly impossible, I shall give you some Reasons why I think it not only lawful in it self, but very necessary in this populous City. And, First, if we consider the Matter that ought to be represented, whether it be Tragedy or Comedy; there is nothing in either that can offend Religion or Good Manners.

Tragedy is a Representation of an Action by some Great Man, teaching us to regulate our Passions with exactness, and by shewing the strange and differing Accidents of Life, to which the most important Persons are subject; proving to us that Vice never goes unpunished; and that true Happiness does not chiefly consist in the Enjoyment of this World.

Comedy is a Representation of common Conversation; and its Design is to represent things Natural; to shew the Faults of Particular Men in order to correct the Faults of the Publick, and to amend the People thro' a fear of being expos'd, with this Observation, That the Ridiculous

culous of the Stage is to be only a Copy of the Ridiculous found in Nature.

In short, 'tis the Property both of Tragedy and Comedy to instruct: The Characters in both are to be Natural; and the Persons concern'd in the whole Action, are to be such whose Vertues ought to provoke us to an Emulation, or whose Vices ought to deter us from imitating their Example. The Language and Sentiments are to be suitable to each Character: A Wise, Good, and Great Man is to say nothing but what is natural for such a one to say: The Gallant Man is to appear with all the Qualities of a Man of Honour: and the Fool in his proper colour'd Coat. The Vices of the Wicked are not to be represented so nicely, as punish'd severely; that is, a Vicious Person is not to be allow'd to plead in favour of his Vices, or to represent his Villany so calmly as to tempt any Man to try Practices in another Place. Vice is only to be brought there to be condemn'd; and the reason of this is, that our Terrour may be excited, and all our Passions vent themselves with Strength and Reason. Our Pity is not to be extended in a wrong place. In short, The Disposition of the Play is to be such that all the Characters have a proper Effect with us. Our Fear, Love, and Anger are to be exerted with Justice; and we are to learn from a just Fable how to behave our selves in earnest. Thus may we exercise our Souls by examining our reasonable Faculties, and try how we can love to extremity,

tremity, and yet without a Fault; to be angry and ſin not; to be juſt without partiality, and rejoyce with them that rejoyce. We are there inſtructed to Love, Hate, and Fear within meaſure, how we may be Men without debaſing our Souls; and all this by moving Examples, which in ſpite of Stubbornneſs, will force its Impreſſions; and 'tis our own Fault if they are not laſting. This certainly muſt recommend the Stage to the Vertuous; and Piety can't be offended at the decent reproving of Vice, and the inſinuating recommendation of Vertue. Here we find Morality urg'd by Precept and Example, and the Stage reprehending thoſe Follies which the Pulpit wou'd bluſh to correct; for tho' the Church is the Place to declaim againſt Sin, yet there are ſome ſorts of Wickedneſs which can't be ſo decently reprov'd there; ſo that the Stage is ſerviceable on this account, to ſupply the Defects of the Pulpit. In ſhort, whatever may be objected againſt the preſent management of the Stage, is of no force againſt ſuch Proceedings as theſe. Religion and Morality can receive no Damage here; for as long as theſe Rules are obſerv'd, they ſtrictly include both.

It was the Opinion of a great Maſter of Reaſon, that Tragedy conduces more to the Inſtruction of Mankind, than even Philoſophy it ſelf, becauſe it teaches the Mind by Senſe, and rectifies the Paſſions by the Paſſions themſelves. And there is this further Advantage, that we have always the Example of great Men before us, and are generally inclinable to take our Manners from them. There has indeed Authorities been produc'd against the Stage, tho' there don't want as ancient Advocates for it; and some of the Fathers themselves writ Plays, however Mr. *Collier* came to forget it.

If the Theatre is capable to give us such Advantage, it will easily be prov'd of what necessity there is for its encouragement in this Populous City: If there were no Politick Reasons, yet the Good to Religion that may be done by it, is a convincing Argument at once for its Lawfulness and Use. I know the Gravity of some can't dispense with so much time to be spent in Diversion; tho' I can't think this a reasonable Objection where so much Profit may attend our Delight. If it be lawful to recreate our selves at all, it can never be amiss to frequent such a Diversion, that only takes up our Time to make us wiser. I wou'd to God all of them were directed to the same End. No Man is to employ himself so as to exclude the Duties of Religion; and there is as much danger in minding too much the Business of the World, as the Pleasures of it; both of them are to be kept within bounds, and both subservient to Religion. The Passions of Men are active and restless; and 'tis the Prudence of every State to encourage some publick Exercise to keep them at quiet. If the Theatre was down, the Churches wou'd not be the fuller for't.

Or

Or if they ſhou'd, Religion is not always the deſign of them who come there; ſo that I cannot ſee that any thing can be allow'd for the publick Diverſion with ſo much Innocence and ſo much Advantage. I'm only afraid that ſuch a Regularity wou'd be too Vertuous for the Age; and I don't doubt but the Beaux and Poetaſters wou'd be full of Exclamation: For it wou'd be a dreadful Time if the Ladies ſhould regard the Play more than their Beaux Airs; and how wou'd *Vanbroug* be able to paſs a Comedy on them, if they ſhou'd once be ſo nice in their Taſte as to diſguſt Obſcenity; this indeed wou'd be a Vexation, and ſuch a Delicacy which Mr. *Congreve* cou'd not be pleaſed with: And if the Town ſhou'd be ſo refin'd to admit of nothing but what is Natural, we can't expect that ever he will gratifie us with another Tragedy. *Durfey* and *Motteux* wou'd write no more Farces; *Guildon* and *Tom. Brown*, *&c.* wou'd be the Saints with wry Mouthes and ſcrue'd Faces: Mr. *Guildon* indeed has Philoſophy enough to ſupport himſelf under ſuch a Calamity, and knows a Method to prevent ſtarving; for who can think that he who writ *Blunt*'s Life can be at a loſs for a decent diſpatch of his own? 'Tis a deplorable Caſe, indeed, and I pity a Man who cannot get Bread by Writing, and yet muſt beg or ſtarve without it.

The Prince of *Conti* believ'd the *French* Stage wou'd not have been ſo bad if the Prieſts had begun ſooner to declaim againſt it: It is poſſible that ſome of our Defects may be owing to

ſuch

ſuch a Negligence. However 'tis never too late to mend ; and ſince Mr. *Collier* has took up the Cudgels, I wiſh the reſt of the ſame Coat wou'd ſo far as is juſt and reaſonable, ſtand his Second : He has his Faults, but they are ſuch as I wou'd not have loſt his Book for. I know there are ſome violent Wits, who will not allow him either Wit or Style, but, in plain terms, to be a Fool. I hope none of them will go about to prove it. I confeſs he has kept ill Company of late ; but ſurely they don't ground a Conjecture upon that, eſpecially when a Man only converſes to convince. The naming Mr. *Durfey*, or examining his Works, is not ſo contagious as to ſtain a Man's Reputation. We are indeed to anſwer for evil Communication ; and tho' I cannot juſtifie a Man who wou'd read Mr. *Durfey* with too much Delight, becauſe we muſt not ſet our Affection on things below, yet I wou'd pardon any who wou'd read him only to forewarm others of the Danger.

'Tis a Misfortune to have good Poets ſtand in need of Aſſiſtance ; but 'tis very much aggravated when they are deny'd it. A Man who is oblig'd to write for his Bread, is forc'd to be very haſty to prevent ſtarving ; And every Man's Genius is not ſo ſharp as his Appetite. This may be one Reaſon we have ſo many things appear Abortive. Some Poets have not ſo much as to ſave their longing ; and if their Muſe miſcarry, or come with an ugly Mark into the World, are rather to be pity'd than condemn'd. In what Pangs have I ſeen ſome poor Creatures

Creatures to be deliver'd, when at the ſame time they have fear'd the Poverty of their Brats, and that the World wou'd diſcover they were very ſick in the breeding. A good Poet ought never to want a worthy Patron; and our Nobility and Gentry ought to be Induſtrious in the Advancement of Letters. They might do it with great eaſe and little Expence; for the Number is not ſo great who deſerve their Countenance. In vain we complain of the Irregularity of the Stage, if they who cou'd ſupport its Honour, want ſupport themſelves: So that one great Step to advance the Theatre, is to take care, that they who write for the Stage, do not want for Encouragement.

You ſee, Sir, I have given my Thoughts freely: I wiſh they may receive your Approbation; becauſe I wou'd never think but to pleaſe you. I dare not now think of excuſing any thing I have writ; for I was reſolv'd to tie my ſelf to no Method, but to think as much as I cou'd for the advantage of the Stage, which I muſt believe very lawful, for any thing I have yet met to the contrary. Nor can I be perſwaded, that our Plays have had ſo ill effect as ſome wou'd imagine. The beſt of our Plays have nothing in them, that is ſo ſcandalous; and for the worſt, I wou'd not allow them the Credit, nor the Authors the Vanity to think they could influence any one Man. The evil Converſation of ſome of them wou'd frighten a Man from being vicious; ſo that they are ſerviceable againſt their Wills, and do the World a Kindneſs through miſtake. I dare not ſtay any longer with you, tho' I have a great Inclination to beg you'd excuſe the roughneſs of my Stile: But you know I have been buſie in *Virgil*; and that they ſay, at *Will's*, is enough to ſpoil it: But if I had begg'd a more important thing, and ask'd you to forgive the length of my Letter, I might aſſure my ſelf you wou'd oblige,

Your Humble Servant.

F I N I S.

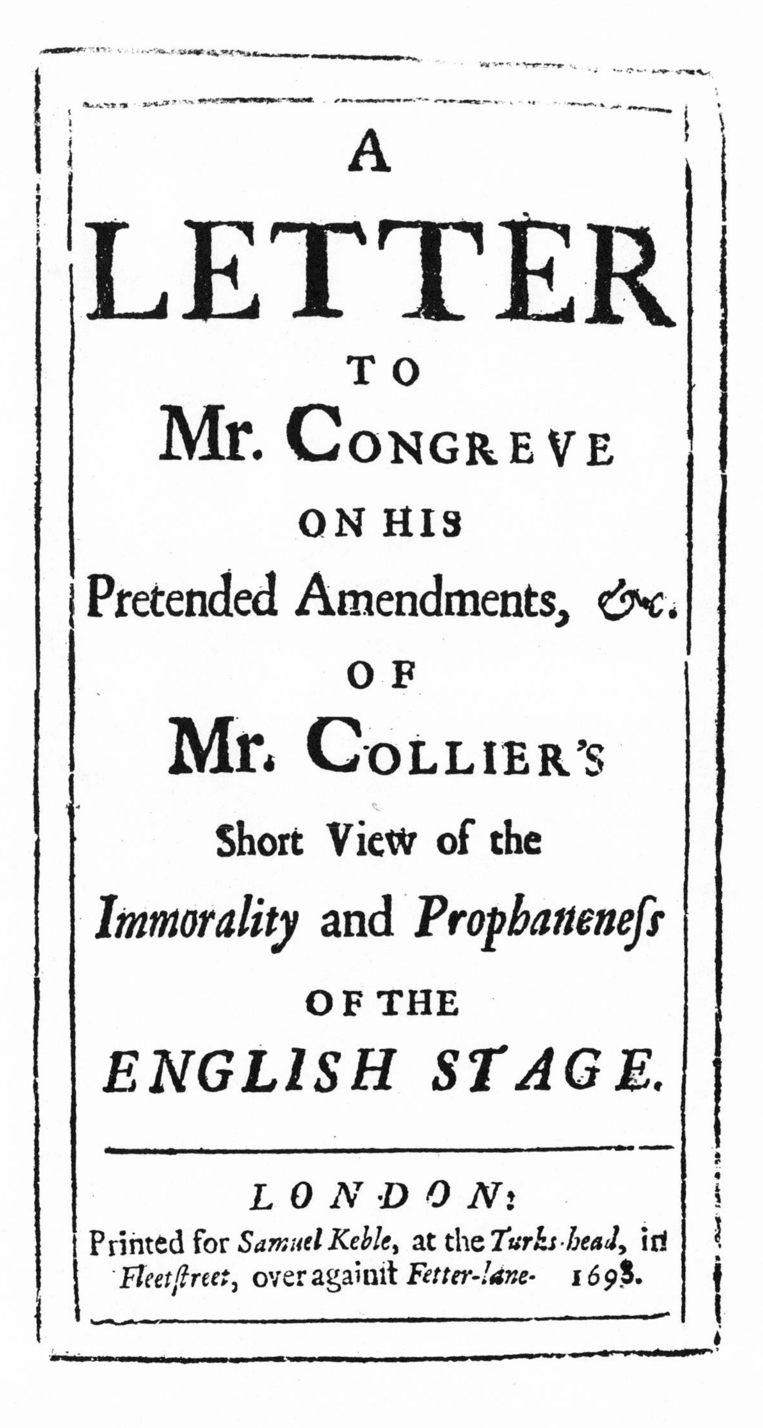

A

LETTER

TO

Mr. CONGREVE

ON HIS

Pretended Amendments, &c.

OF

Mr. COLLIER'S

Short View of the

Immorality and *Prophaneness*

OF THE

ENGLISH STAGE.

LONDON:

Printed for *Samuel Keble*, at the *Turks-head*, in *Fleetstreet*, over against *Fetter-lane*. 1698.

A LETTER TO Mr. *Congreve*, On his pretended Amendments, &c.

SIR,

TO be thought *Lazy*, I must confess, is not much for ones credit; and you have shewn, that to take pains to be *Idle*, is as little worth ones while: So that if you had no other reason to write against Mr. *Collier*, than to avoid the Scandal of *Lazyness*; you must not be angry if I call it a very *Idle* Answer.

P. 2.

 You

You ſay, *you would not undertake to defend the Corruptions of the Stage* ; not while you write Comedies for it, I judge: but if it will not, by your own confeſſion, bear a *defence* ; I am ſure, you ſhould *undertake* to reform it : your place, and intereſt in it, do more eſpecially oblige you to it: and if Mr. *Collier* had laid the wickedneſs of a great many more Plays, beſides your own, at your door, he had not much abus'd you; becauſe they muſt have your approbation, before they come upon that Stage, to which you are related : which perhaps might put that Gentleman upon dealing a little more ſevere with you than ordinary.

I am ſorry I cannot think you altogether ſo innocent, and ſo good a Chriſtian, as you ſhould be ; but yet you need not fall abſolutely into deſpair ; you are not, you ſee, denied *the benefit of the Clergy*: Mr. *Collier*, whoſe hard fate it is, to be moſt at leiſure for your *Ordinary*; has beſtowed a great deal of good pains upon you : but really you have ſo very foully, and ungraciouſly requited him ; that, I am afraid, he will

P. 3.

ſcarce

ſcarce think it worth his while, to be at any more trouble about you; if you are ſo hardened, and recoyling, he muſt e'en give you over.

I had thoughts, to put all your dirty, and *Billings-gate* language, againſt him, into one Paragraph; and had heapt it up together, as well as I could, for ſuch an unreaſonable quantity, in ſo little a compaſs; but, when I had done, I found, I had in effect, copied your whole Book; there were only a few impertinent, and ſenſeleſs lines left, ſcarce worth obſervation; and then, it made ſuch a loathſome *Dunghil*, as you call it, that I was forced to hold my Noſe; and away with it.

You fall Egregiouſly foul, both upon his Intellectuals, and his Morals; you have endeavoured to detect Mr. *Collier*, to be a man of great *abſurdity*, and *ignorance*. Now, he that makes ſo very bold with another, ought, in prudence and good manners, to be ſome conſiderable degrees above him, both in Virtue and in Senſe: but when I compare the ſeveral *Eſſay*'s that Gentleman has given, of his Judgment, and penetration,

P. 2.

with your *four poor Plays*, I cannot think the right lay on your ſide, to render him ſo contemptible for his Ignorance.

You repreſent him, from cover to cover, for a moſt notoriouſly lewd, and immoral man, a perſon *in the high Vigour of obſcenity*; and you have a pretty way with you to keep up his Character, when you beſtow ſo many damnable, lewd allegories on him, in your Anſwer: He *commits a rape upon your words*, and that you heighten ſtill, to be no leſs than *deflowring of Virgins*: There is, indeed, ſuch a deal of *Virginity* belonging to the Stage, every way, that any one who breaks in upon you, is in danger of being laid hold on for a *Raviſher*.

p. 4.

I muſt ſtep forward a little, to mind you here; that you ſay, *Metaphors do chiefly diſtinguiſh, the manner of a mans Breeding, and Converſation*; and, *that ſuch Ideas, have their beginning, from a familiarity with ſuch objects*: Why, what a Beaſt will you make of your ſelf, at this rate of arguing? *committing a rape upon words*; *Raviſhing the Virgins*; *looking on naked obſcenity*, and then *Flogging* out; (I thank God, I am Ignorant

p. 85.

what

what Idea you have to match with that word:) The next that follows, of a *ſinful Pædagogue*, is almoſt Sodomitical; and then after all this, *licking himſelf whole with an abſolution.* Examin your ſelf a little; by ſuch original Images of yours, as theſe, and then conſider, whether you have right on your ſide, to fall ſo very foul on Mr. *Collier's* Morals; unleſs it happens to be with you, as Sir *Roger L'Eſtrange* obſerves it was with one of the *lewdeſt Strumpets*, to be always crying out, *Lord, to ſee the Impudence of ſome Women!*

But Mr. *Collier* was not an Idiot, when he ſet his name to his Book: If he had been conſcious to himſelf, of any conſiderable immorality, when he did it; he muſt have been abandoned: He knew what Adverſaries he was going to create; but *innocency is bold as a Lyon:* And I do not find, either that Mr. *Dennis*, who ſate at the head of a Club, above a Month to impeach him, or Mr. *Congreve*, who has ſtaid longer upon the Inquiſition, have laid any one conſiderable inſtance of Immorality to his charge, except it be the writing of a very ingenious book againſt it.

You

P. 4. You represent him for an *evil Spirit* entring into your Plays: Now *evil Spirits* have shewn a very great alacrity and inclination, at entring into any thing that is *Swinish*: Therefore, I cannot blame you for taking alarm at the word *Legion*, in relation to your own little Herd: But really, you had no reason to apprehend Mr. *Collier* for that Trespass; for his only fault is, he did not go into them so far as he should have done, to do you Justice: He has happen'd to fall foulest upon your *Mourning Bride*; which, being least liable to Exception, he could endure to read over; but he has been very spairing of the *three biggest* for Obscenity, and Prophaneness; which is the greatest advantage he has given you against him.

P. 6. You say again, you *will take the liberty to whip the evil Spirit out of your Plays, wherever you can meet him*. I am glad of that withal my Heart. But be advised; whip the Devil gently; you don't know, but it may come to his turn, to favour you another time: If

Ib. Mr. *Collier* has returned any of your *current* Cash *into the Devil's Exchequer* for you, it will be ready for you, against

you

you have occasion for an Interest there.

You seem to be in pain, and remorse, with your self, that you have not duly *return'd his Civilities, in calling him Names*: But be out of pain; you have done pretty well, for a Gentleman: And, I believe, I have a Collection of yours, out of this short Essay, that will be a Match for Mr. *Collier's Nomenclature*, at any time: Beside, when it seem'd to run low with you, his own Personal Names, *Jeremy* and *Collier*, proved great helps to you.

I am now come to your *Postulata*.

The first I grant you, because 'tis *Aristotles*, and a Just one. The second I must refuse you, that is your own, and Unreasonable: You ought not to represent any Immoralities upon the Stage, either in Word, or Deed, that will give Offence to chaste and sober Ears, no, tho you pretend to punish them afterwards: You might as well argue, it would be of use to have idle Fellows Swear and Curse in the Streets, purely for the sake of giving sober Men, an opportunity to Chide them: We are offended much at such things from the Persons

P. 7.
P. 9.

themselves; and much more, when we have them represented to us, with advantages at second hand. You say, *it were very hard, a Painter should be thought to resemble all the the ugly Faces he draws*; [remember here again your Doctrine of *Ideas*.] But what if a *Painter* chooses to draw Obscene, and Baudy Pieces, and exposes them to the Publick, for their Diversion; is it hard that such a one should be Censured? Or, can we think, his Thoughts were altogether so chastly taken up, and employ'd, when they were directing the Pencil?

Ibid. Your Third I grant you, tho your own; nor do I expect Thanks for the favour, because I think 'tis very indifferent, whether your *Passages* are read in *Collier* or your self: There are but too words odds that I can find, and they are *wasting*, for *wafting*; and the little word, *still*, omitted: Only, if we must needs look back *into the Field of Nature, from whence they were transplanted*; we shall have a larger *Field* of Debauchery to walk in, and a great deal of worse Stuff, than Mr. *Collier* has Collected still in view.

P. 27. P. 47. P. 4.

If

If you demand the priviledge of the *Habeas Corpus Act*, to remove your offensive Plays, from the *Quarter-Sessions of Middlesex*, to the *King's-Bench Bar*; and appeal from the *Presentment of the Grand Jury*, to a *just Judge*; I believe the thing may be practicable enough, but I queston whether it would do you any Service.

I must differ with you a little again, about your fourth *Postulatum*. [You should be advised, Mr. *Congreve*, when you chose this odd way of vindicating Poems Mathematically; to see that your Principles be self-evident: But you shew your self so needy, and ask such unreasonable things, and with that Confidence, that you will be taken notice of, by all the *Philomaths in and about* London, for a sturdy Beggar in their way.] *When words*, you say, *are applied to Sacred things, and with a purpose to treat of Sacred things, they ought to be understood accordingly*: Right! and so they ought. *But when they are otherwise applied, the diversity of the Subject, gives them a diversity of signification*: Right again! That is to say, in the former case, they are *sacredly* uſed; but when the ſame peculiar words are taken, and uſed in this latter caſe, which is yours, they are uſed *Prophanely*; and is the Sin that is commonly expreſs'd by that Phraſe, *ludere cum Sacris*: And now, what ſervice can you expect from a Propoſition, that is already Revolted from you? I muſt tell you, there is a great deal of difference, between uſing the ſame common *Alphabet*, with that in Scripture; and the borrowing of ſome peculiar Words, or Phraſes, from it, that are *ſpelt out of that Alphabet*. For Example, our Saviour has this peculiar Expreſſion of himſelf, **I am the Truth**; which is ſo emphatical, and remarkable, in relation to his Perſon, that the whole tenor of the Goſpel depends upon it: When this Expreſſion therefore is put familiarly into the Mouth of a Mad-man upon the Stage, and made as it were, the diſtinguiſhing Catch, and Bob of his Frenzy; this I think, is ſomething more, than ſpelling out of the *Alphabet*. I do aſſure you, it had that ill effect, that I never met with any one, who came from that Play, but confeſt, it gave them Offence; and

and minded them from whom the expreſſion was taken. Wou'd you had
been contented with your firſt thought,
I am *Tom tell troth*! for that had been
harmleſs, and fooliſh enough, and fit
for a Mad-man.

Having ended your *Poſtulata*, and
made ſuch an Apology, as was neceſſary, for the *latitude* they be ſpeak:
you proceed to ſubjoin a ſort of *Hypo-
theſis*, of the *moral inſtruction of Plays*,
to this purpoſe: That when the *Play is
over*, we have all the moral of it,
ſumm'd up in a few lines to the Audience, *in Rhyme, to be more engaging
upon the memory*: for example, *In Love
for Love*; the moral of it is ſumm'd up
very briefly in that Diſtick, at the
cloſe.

The miſtery this day is, that we find,
A Lover true; not that a Womans kind.

here, you have the whole Moral of a
long Play, wrapt up at laſt, in a *miſtery*, for the better inſtruction of the
Audience.

I ſee no great occaſion of moderating diſtinctly, between you both, in relation to all the particular matters in diſpute, from your Plays: Your *Tragedy* is a very good one, and Anſwers Sir *Rich. Blackmores* Character of it, who recommends it, for an admirable one; but ſtill with this reſerve, *ſome few things only excepted*: for inſtance; when you make King *Manuel*, in the fury of his reſentment, ſay, of *Oſmyns pleading audacious Love* to his Miſtreſs;

Preface to King *Ar.*

Mourn. Bride p. 26.

Better for him, to tempt the rage of Heaven,
And wrench the bolt red-hiſſing, from the hand
Of him that thunders,————
'Tis daring for a God.———

Thats a bold ſtroke indeed! I proteſt, if I had been the Author of it, I ſhould have trembled at the *Gigantick* inſolence of my fancy: afterward, the attempt is likened to *Ixions Embracing Divinity*: Bleſs me! you Poets do frequently make ſo bold with God Almighty, and his Divinity; that if he had

had not declared himſelf, from his own mouth, to be a God of Patience and long ſuffering; I ſhould wonder how he does bear it of you.

Then again, you make this bluſtering King pay his, and your reſpects, to the Character, and Office of a Clergyman, very handſomely.

I'll have a Prieſt ſhall preach her from her faith,
And make it ſin, not to renounce that vow,
Which I'd have broken.

Mourning Bride, p. 10.

But when you make ſo very bold with God's honour, his Prieſts may contentedly take any thing, in the ſame Play: *The Diſciple is not above his Maſter, nor the Servant above his Lord, &c.* vid. Matt. 10. 24, 25, 26.

I would fain beſtow one note more upon the *Mourning Bride*, tho' I am ſure to incur the Cenſure of ill nature, and the *Splene* for it: This I know is your Darling Off-ſpring, and therefore I would be very tender of it; you have been at the expence of more Education than ordinary upon it, and

therefore

therefore you say, p. 25, *If Smut, and Prophaneness, can be prov'd against this, you must give up the Cause.* I am not now upon charging it with *Smut*; but when I have dropt this one remark more to the two former, I will leave it to your self to judge, whether it is not now and then a little *Prophane*: Methinks you seem somewhat Conscious of it already; when immediately after, in that same Paragraph, you silently let fall the word *Prophaneness*; and cry out, *if there be immodesty in that Tragedy, I must confess my self incapable of ever writing any thing with modesty, or decency.*

But to convince you farther (if you are not yet convinc't) that there is *Prophaneness* in that Play, let me prevail with you to weigh that violent rapture of *Osmyn* to his *Bride* over again. *Mourn. Bride*, p. 35.

My all of bliss, my everlasting Life,
Soul of my Soul, and end of all my wishes.

Osmyn, or *Alphonso*, is your *Hero*; and design'd for the Character of a very

very good, and brave Person; and therefore, when it comes to his turn to speak, we expect a great deal of the *Poets* mind, and Principles from him; for the Honourable * Mr. *Granville*, makes it *a pretty true observation of Poets, that in the frame of their Heroes, they commonly draw their own Pictures*: But now, when *your All of bliss, Your everlasting life, Your very Soul,* and *the end of all your wishes,* are all wrapt up together, and consummated in the enjoyment of one Woman; What is become of your *Heaven?* Or what farther business, or interest can you have depending in that *eternal* state, where *they neither Marry, nor are given in Marriage?* I am clearly for your encouraging Men to Love their Wives; but there is no necessity of representing a Good Husband so very *uxorious*, as to make him declare himself possest of *Heaven*, and the *eternal rewards of Religion*, when he has his *Spouse* in his Arms.——— But some grains of allowance must be made here, since

* Preface to Heroick Love.

This was an Off'ring to the sex design'd. Epil.

After all, allowing your Adverſary has been a little too angry with that Celebrated Tragedy of yours; Would you have your Comedies paſs without exception too? What think you of your *Prologue* to the *Double Dealer*? where you would inſinuate, by the alluſion of a *Mooriſh Cuſtom*, that there's hardly a Husband in all the City of *London*, but what's a *Cuckold*: and, the better to grace them in that Character, you are pleas'd to give them the venerable Epethite of, *Chriſtian Cuckolds*.

I'th Good Man's Arms, the Chopping baſtard thrives,
For he thinks all his own, that is his Wives.

I am ſure it ought to be ſo, and to inſinuate the contrary, is to ſtir up Jealouſie; which is evidently the deſign of the whole Play that follows. On this occaſion, be ſo kind to lend me the two firſt Verſes of your *Prologue* to the old *Batchelour*.

How this vile World is chang'd! in former days,

Pro-

Prologues, were serious Speeches, before Plays;
Grave solemn things,——

p. 56.

There is your own Confession, to one great part of Mr. *Collier*'s Book, how infinitely the *Antients* exceeded our *Modern* pretenders to Poetry, in the *Gravity*, and *Morality* of their performances.

In short, if *Belinda*, and *Letitia*, in the old *Batch.* If *the three biggest*, of the four Women in the *Double Dealer*, have their Characters, and Cues, contrived for the advancement of Modesty, and Virtue; If, in *Love for Love*, *Tattle*'s instructing of *Miss Prue*, and her saying her *Catechism* after him, wherein she is taught a little of Mr. *Congreve*'s *Court breeding*; To give up her Virtue, *and to lye, to be angry, and yet more complying; to fall back, when she should run away; and to hold her tongue, when she should cry out*; And, if Mrs. *Foresights* leaving them together, to do their worst, in that juncture, were intended *out of good morality*; then some well meaning People have been very much mistaken, that's all.

You frequently take occasion to Triumph, and Lord it over Mr. *Collier*, in point of *Criticism*; 'tis your Province, I confess, more than his; and therefore, if you are the greater Master in that Art, it is no such wonder; but I think Impartially, you come short of him in your own Business, and that is a thing to be wondred at indeed. At least, you are pleas'd to shew your self a *sowre Critick*, when you have no ground: You quarrel at Mr. *Collier*'s Phrase of *learning a Spaniel to Set*; which shews, that you are yet to *learn* the compass of our English Tongue, or that you are resolved to be a Wrangling, right or wrong. Say you, *I suppose, he means*, teaching *a Spaniel to Set*. But why so? What necessity is there for changing the Word, only to put as good a one in the place? For, is Mr. *Congreve* yet to be told, that *to learn*, is often used Actively, for *to teach*? Does he not remember it to be so used in the *Psalter*? *O learn me true Understanding*! I chuse to refer you to that Ejaculation, because it may be a proper one for you, to use in your Devotions.

In

In *p*. 32, you alarm'd me of ſomething very dreadful in that Expreſſion of Mr. *Collier*'s, *Nature made the ferment and riſing of the Blood, for ſuch occaſions*: But, having turn'd to his Book for it, I am now at a loſs, which to queſtion moſt, your *Underſtanding* or *Sincerity*, in that Charge: I hope, ſay you, *he ſpeaks Figuratively*; as 'tis plain he does, for it is a ſort of *Metonimy*: And yet in the next Paragraph, you take him *Literally*, and endeavour to make mad work with it; but it will not ſerve your turn that way: And if it be *Figuratively*, ſaid, I perceive you have nothing to ſay to it. Take it and turn it how you pleaſe; I am ſure you cannot make it look *Prophanely*: For, allowing *Nature* there to ſignify our *Maker*, which is the utmoſt you would have; then to ſay, Nature *made the ferment of our Blood, for ſuch Occaſions*; is, in Mr. *Collier*'s Senſe, to ſay, That *God made the riſing of our Paſſions on purpoſe*, to ſhew our reſentment againſt bad Plays, and ſuch like ſinful Provocations: Which I think, is very wiſely and juſtly ſaid; And your quarrelling ſo lamentably with it, ſerves only to ſhew what you would

would be at, and no more: Unless you will give me leave to observe from thence, how wretchedly you are out of the way, and lost, when you put your self upon talking *Savoury* and *Religiously*. You must not be angry, if I take this occasion, of turning the *but-end* of a quaint expression of your own, against you; *The Corruption of a Rotten-Poet, is the Generation of a very sowre, and aukward Divine.* Writers you see, will be free with one another, and borrow, and pay upon occasion.

P. 26.

Over leaf we have you in another fit of *Divinity* again; I am glad to find it; 'tis a good sign: And tho' you are still very aukward at it, there's hopes you may improve; 'tis but young dayes with you in that profession: You should let alone St. *Chrysostom* yet; 'tis a vanity with all young Divines, to be nibling and retailing the Fathers, before they are well grounded in the Bible. St. *Chrysostom's* rule, as you have apply'd it, will signify nothing: For did not God command the Prophet *Isaiah*, to *Cry aloud, and spare not*, and *to lift up his voice like a Trumpet.* And yet for all that *Tumult*, you must own, if you set

Isa. 68. 1.

ſet up for a Divine, that he was *inſpir'd with the Holy Ghoſt* : *So*, you ſee, *now the reaſon is* not ſo *plain* again.

I would now march forward with you, and Juſtify the Charges of Prophaneneſs, and Smut, that are exhibited againſt you; and, to do you any good, would produce a great many more, which your Adverſary has omitted: But the miſchief of it lyes here; If Mr. *Collier* paſt any of it over, out of Modeſty, with a Daſh, as being too Baudy to be expreſs'd; then you cry, *it lyes yet upon him to prove it*; *his bare Aſſertion without an Inſtance, is not ſufficient*: And if he diſobliges his Paper with a little of it expreſly, to prove *downright ſmut* upon you, then all your Thanks is, *why e'en let him take it for his pains*: And with either one, or the other *horn* of this *Dilemma*, I find you moſt commonly upon your defence: The force, and weight of your whole Vindication, ſeems very much to depend upon this Argument: And, to ſay truth, it is, as you have pitch'd, and fortified it, an impregnable one: But who, do you think, will be at the pains to help you cleanſe your Plays of their

P. 43.

their *Smut*, and *Filthineſs*, when you will only allow him to carry off the *Dung* for his labour? Indeed, when you ſay, *you are willing to part with it*, you come up to our terms; but you ſoon relapſe again; there is no holding you to your Bargain.

When Mr. *Collier* charges you with prophaning the word *Inſpiration*, your Anſwer is, *The poor Man is troubled with the Flatus, his Spleen is puſt up with Wind; and* then the conſequence is, *he is likely to grow very Angry and Peeviſh on the ſuddain; and deſires the priviledge to ſcold and give it vent.* Now, if the *Spleen* had not taken poſſeſſion of all your Underſtanding, and Senſe, you would never have confeſs'd this to be the natural effect and and product of that Diſeaſe: For, do not we know that you are almoſt devoured with it? That you have no other Excuſe, but that, for the preſent ſullen dulneſs, and ſtupidity of your Converſation? That you have no other Excuſe for writing ſuch a Book as this? That 'tis impoſſible you ſhould write ſuch a one without it? If it were not for the Credit of a *Poet*, to keep you

P. 45.

you a little in countenance, you would find your ſelf perfectly abandoned for your *Spleen*, by all ingenious Society: And yet, it ſeems, you could think your ſelf qualified to charge the *Flatus*, with all its ſcurvey effects upon Mr. *Collier*, out of meer diſdain. Well, I ſee, being related to the Play-houſe will furniſh a man in time, with a ſurmounting aſſurance, that will ſtick at nothing. But, before I part with you about this *Diſeaſe*, let me adviſe you to examine the *Symptoms* of it ſeriouſly with your ſelf, for it is a very equivocal one; many times, when we would ſeem to impute the fault to our *Spleen*, or *Hypochondria*, it really lyes in the Conſcience, and is nothing elſe but an over bearing weight of guilt in the Mind.

The reaſon why I lodge this caution with you, is, becauſe you are not afraid to publiſh very ill *Symptoms* of your caſe to the World: For, would any one but a very looſe and immoral man, have choſen *to amuſe himſelf in a ſlow recovery from a fit of ſickneſs*, by writing of an obſcene Play? Would any one have thought

P. 39.

thought upon that occasion of writing of It, to help to excuse the obscenity? And, to shew your Repentance for the same, set up a Horse laugh at the beginning of a Paragraph, that concern'd your Conscience so nearly? A good Christian, I am sure, would have chosen to turn his meditations quite another way, on such a juncture. At this rate, what ever you dye a *Martyr* for, it will not be for your *Religion*: But you have distinguisht upon the word, and told us there are *Martyrs* of several sorts: Mr. *Collier* you say, *is a Martyr to scandal*; 'tis well 'tis no worse, for *Martyrs* you know, are alwayes supposed to suffer unjustly: But there is yet another sort of *Martyr* you mentioned, far beyond that; which in your condition you cannot be too much aware of, and that is, to be a *wicked Martyr*, *or Martyr for the Devil*.

P. 48.

You strive hard to bring off that expression of yours, That *Nature has been provident only to Bears, and Spiders*; but supposing I should return your dealing with Mr. *Collier* upon the same word, and

P. 51.

and change *Nature* into *God*, the Author of It; then the expression would be, *God has been provident only to Bears and Spiders:* This, you must needs think, would not sound altogether so well.

P. 31.

What follows in the three next Pages is to publish your great reading in *Judicial Astrology*; which I shall make no exceptions against, but advice you to bend your studys that way; you may be more serviceable to the publick therein, than by writing some sort of Plays, if it be only by being more Innocent.

You so often Triumph at Mr, *Collier's Absolutions*, that I can't choose but take notice of it; you don't consider what a very mean, and contemptable man you appear your self while you strut and crow thus over anothers misfortunes; it has been alwayes taken for the mark of a base, and ungenerous mind: But if that Gentleman has been so unfortunate in dispencing his *Absolution* once, he will be more wary for the future; and endure a great deal of *pounding*, as you call it, before he will yield to pro-

P. 77.

ſtitute his Office ſo far, as to ſquander a-way an *Abſolution* upon any one belong-ing to the Stage.

P. 60. You mount in your defence hugely, concerning the Clergy; and having ſmelt at your Adverſaries Argu-ments, you deſpiſe them ; and march along in Triumph for a many Pages and carry it with ſuch a high hand, and lay about you ſo furiouſly;that it is hard-ly ſafe for a ſtander by to ſtep in, and interrupt you : However, when you have paſt Mr. *Collier* quite through, and clincht him; you will not be angry, if out of meer compaſſion, I cloſe in with you, and hold your arm, to parle a little in his behalf: At the *upper end* of P. 72. *ditto*, one may plainly per-ceive your ſtorm coming on apace; the *Poet* breaks the poor *Prieſts* line in peices, and paſſes thick upon him: Therefore yet I will ſtand aloof.

Prieſt——*In fine, the Play is a very Religious Poem.*

Poet, Indeed!
loquitur.

Prieſt

Prieſt,——*'Tis upon the matter all Ser-mon and Anthem.*——————

Poet, O Lord!

Prieſt,——*And if it were not deſign'd for the Theater*——————

Poet, Out with it man.

Prieſt,——*I have nothing to object*.

So *that's well*, there is one tough bout over, *O' my word I was half afraid* how matters would have gone: But the *Poet* over leaf, owns *this will not doe; the advantage does not yet appear:* Therefore ſtand clear again.

Poet, No! Why then

Prieſt,——*He is rewarded by the King*.

Here's another breathing again; this bout was but very ſhort, and the Poet yet confeſſes, that *the advantage does appear ſtill but coldly.* But ſtand off once more, and beware of the third time——————

Poet, Ay? Say you ſo? Why then——————

Prieſt

Prieſt,——*In ſhort*————

Poet, Ay ? now for the Iliads in a Nutt-ſhell. Ah !--Ah ?——Now the *But's* coming indeed, *I had a glimps of him but juſt now.*

Prieſt, *In ſhort he is repreſented lewd but not little.*

Poet——There's an advantage for you now; *In ſhort*, Lewd *but not* little..

And here Mr. *Collier*, poor man is ſuppoſed to fall: I will therefore now ſtep in and examine whether his wound be mortal, or no; for it ſeems 'twas a home thruſt.————Hah? Why is this all the execution ? Here's one of *Hudibras's* notable Combats; a huge clattering, and coyle, but nothing done.—*Lewd*, but not *little*: If that be all, I'll fetch but two Small Stitches, and it ſhall be as ſound a Limb, as any Mr. *Congreve* has about him. Let me ſee—*Lewd*, as to his Perſon; but not *little*, as to his Office. There, now 'tis done. This is plainly Mr. *Collier's* meaning

meaning, and all he contends for, in ſo many Pages before, where he is ſo ſtrangely put to the banter.

Well, but ſay you, *then, I confeſs, I have been in an errour*: Why is that ſuch a wonder? But ſtill I ſee you will miſtake your ſelf; for this once you are in the right: You ſay, *I thought a man never appeared ſo little, as when he appear'd extreamly Lewd*, 'tis true; but then, keep the man, and his function aſſunder; and, as Mr. *Collier* explained himſelf in the ſame breath (where you ſo diſingeniouſly, and Barbarouſly interrupted him to ſhew your little wit:) *The diſ-falls rather upon the perſon than the office.*

P. 71

For, as he explains himſelf in ano- place, p. 139. the *Man* may be *little*; but the *Prieſts* are not ſo. Contrary whereunto, he has ſufficiently ſhewn, *Chap.* 4. you contrive your *Lewd* men and *Rakes*, to make the moſt conſiderable Figures in your Comedy: Which ſhews, how little uſe you make of a good *Thought*, in your way of *Practice*

Where-

Whereas you give your audience no other opportunity of judging of the dignity of a *Prieſt's* office, but by letting them ſee a man in holy Orders, always in the very meaneſt Character; and Condition; ſneaking, and contemptable, to the loweſt degree of Comedy, and reducing *Rogers* Reverence, underneath the favours of a *Nurſe*.

But let me get out of all this ſtuff once, and come with you to the merits of the cauſe; which if I intend to do I muſt meet you at your Concluſion of this Head, p. 86. *I will only ſay, that no man living has a greater reſpect for a good Clergy Man, than my ſelf*; Let all that are good of the Order, riſe up and thank you for it! But what method do you take to manifeſt your reſpect to them? Why truly, by never bringing a Clergy-man on the Stage, but in a ridiculous manner: and conſequently, you never take an occaſion to put your audience in mind of one of that order; but to expoſe him to contempt: all your *Parſons* are brought in upon baſe, and ſordid errands; which nothing can

P. 86.

juſtifie

justifie in you, but the supposition, that all of them are really of that Stamp and Character; which truely is very hard: In the mean time, you never take any care to distinguish the ill man from his office, by any reserve of Reverence to it; nor drop any thing that shall give your Audience the least occasion to remember, that the Order, and good Professors of it are absolutely unconcerned in the *Buffoon's* part upon the Stage.

You say, you are *very indifferent, whether ever the Gown appear upon the Stage, or not*: would you had put a full period there! *but*, say you, *if it does, it should not be worn by the Character of a good Man*: That's a strange relaps of kindness to them indeed. Why? would it look like such an unnatural representation, to shew that *Gown* on a *Good Mans* back? I must be very short with you upon this point; all the whole World, without the Play-house doors, who have any regard for Religion, are against you in this matter : and that upon very good reaſon, founded upon experience, that will not endure to be contradicted: for the People are apt enough to be miſlead into an ill opinion of the Clergy of themſelves ; and therefore, when you always ſhew the *Parſon* in a ridiculous manner, they will be apt to take the hint, and without diſtinction, think a *Parſon* ridiculous: and while they are tempted to have the Clergy in deriſion, the next ſhort ſtep that immediately follows, will be to have Religion ſo too.

A *Poet* had need call himſelf an *Ally* to the Clergy at this rate: You ſhew your ſelf in another form in the foregoing Paragraph; there you appear without diſguiſe, as inveterate an Enemy to that Order, for the compaſs of one Section, as ever I met with in my Life. You there take an occaſion from Mr. *Colliers* Book, to ſeduce the whole *Laity* againſt the *Clergy*, and hoot them about their ears. *I am not the only one*, ſay you

you, *who look upon this Pamphlet of his, to be a gun level'd at the whole Laity, while the ſhot only glances on the Theatre* : I am ſorry it only *glances* there, I believe all the force of it was intended to be ſpent intirely on it: And I believe, out of the *Theatre*, Mr. *Congreve* is the only man who would have the *gun* to be *level'd at the whole Laity*. He can have but one Argument on his ſide, to give him countenance, and that he prepared for himſelf, againſt he ſhould be in diſtreſs: In the 16. P. of his Book. It runs, in ſhort, to this effect; The *Stage* repreſents the *whole World*, this *great gun* was *level'd* directly *againſt the Stage*, ſo, againſt the whole World: And, by conſequence it did but juſt *glance* upon the Stage, but fell in with the whole *Laity* and made mad work with them. But now, if you will give me leave, I will remind you of one plain reaſon grounded upon matter of fact that the whole *Laity* did not take this *gun* to be *level'd directly against them*; for, if you remember, assoon as ever it was discharged against the *Theatre*, they took it for a signal to fall upon you, and accordingly, the next *Quarter Sessions*, *the Grand Jury of Middlesex* (as I hinted before) who are all *Lay-men*, presented Mr. *Congreve* and some others, for their obscene Plays. I shall not take notice of the further respect you shew the Clergy there, where you open a whole Field of War against them, for their *Controversial Divinity*.

For my part, I declare, I am a Friend to Religion, and no Enemy to good Poetry; if you take care to maintain your *alliance* to the Clergy, by having a due regard to their Character, and Cause. I shall think the Stage no unjustifiable diversion, and amusement, to People. A celebrated Female in use, has lately convinc'd you, in her *fatal Friendship*, that 'tis possible

Mrs. Trotter.

possible to entertain, with all the Judgment, Wit, and Beauty of Poetry; without *shocking our senses*, with intollerable prophaness or obscenity

There is nothing, I know, which you affect more, than to pass for a fine, and exact Writer, even to a Mathematical nicety! but I must speak freely, I never could yet meet with a Dramatick Poet that could write good Prose. Your Essays that way do commonly dwindle, and run off into Dialogism, Ramble, and Banter; thus, at every short turn of your pen, *Indeed! O Lord! Ay? your Servant*; *&c.* Even Mr. *Congreve* himself is as far from being a Correct, and steady Oratour, as *Tully* was from being a good Poet: To convince you of this, I shall not stand with you for a deal of absurd trifling, and awkard stuff, that puts the Reader out of countenance, and sickens his taste, and apprehension, almost in every Page of your little Book: But

But before I take my leave of you for the present, I shall just point out to your Eye, a few of those obvious and blazing inconsistencies (I had well nigh said Contradictions) which you have so plentifully dropt in, among your Amendments of Mr. *Collier's* faults, *ex. gr.*

P. 77. You charge him severely for *frequenting* the Play-house: *Why does he abandon*, &c. *And come capering, and frisking between the Scenes?* And yet, P. 109, you insinuate him to be a Man of *Conspiracy*, and *Sedition*; and at the same time impute the cause of it, to the non-frequenting of *Theatres*, and *Musick.*—— But this, you will say, was a great many Pages asunder.———Well,

But, P. 104, you first charge Mr. *Collier* for his *share in the Vanity of triumphing in the worst Argument*; and yet in the very same line you say, *I think truly he had a fair appearance of right on his side.*——

This

This fell out very unhappily indeed.

P. 99. you ſay, *you wonder he is not aſhamed to own that he is ſo well acquainted with the* ἐκκλησιαζούσαι *of Ariſtophanes*; and yet but ſix lines after you confeſs, as if he *meant to veil* that Play under a *Miſnomer*: And again, that by his *Artifice* he *deſign'd* not to *be diſcovered.* By the way, if it were ſuch an abominable ſhame to own the reading of that Play, How came the baſhful, and ſhame-fac'd Mr. *Congreve* to publiſh in the ſame breath, how very intimately he has been acquainted with it himſelf? So far it ſeems, as to Epitomize all the Obſcenity of it, and to compute with *little Bays*, how many times *he names the thing directly*: by your remarks it comes to a *hundred* and odd, and your word truly is to be taken in ſuch a caſe; for I believe you would not willingly have overlook'd any Idea tending that way, for want of application:

plication: And in ſo doing, by your own argument, you have well imploy'd your time, and your imagination: Nothing can bring you off handſomly from this pinch; but putting on a bold face, and owning, that it is peculiarly your buſineſs to read baudy, as well as write it. There is no neceſſity I muſt confeſs, that a *Poet* ſhould be aſhamed of every thing which other men ought to be aſham'd off. But to go on,

P. 93. You declare, *you have avoided all recriminations*: And yet, your whole Book is little elſe, but an attempt at recrimination upon Mr. *Collier* throughout.

Once more, In the ſame Paragraph you ſay, *you have not ſo much as made one Citation from any of your Plays in favour of them*; and yet, P. 22. and 23, you tranſcribe all the Moral of the *Double dealer*, *i.e.* all that is tollerable of the whole Play, to bring it off,

if

if you can, from being guilty of *running riot upon Smut and Pedantry*. And again P. 36. you particularly point out the chief of those parts of the *Mourning Bride*, which are worthy to be observed, in order to have them attone for *one or two erroneous expressions* in it. I have not leisure to compare you any farther with your self, but these few instances of varience between you, are sufficient to convince you, that the next time you write in an angry Controversie, you should make use of more sincerity, or at least a better memory.

After all, I don't find that Mr. *Collier*, or any body else, but one poor *Old Woman* could ever bring you to confess, and reform an errour, or do any good upon you: She, (God knows who or whence!) one out of the Clouds 'tis like, for you have lost her direction, and cannot remember) she, once it seems, convinc't you of a fault, which you candidly acknowledge,

P. 42. and there promiſe to *ſtrike it out in the next impreſſion*: when the *Double Dealer* has another Edition, I believe you may be as good as your word: by that time perhaps you may think of mending ſome other faults of yours, that more nearly concern your Perſon. You will take this freedom, I hope, in good part, from one who is with all due reſpects, *&c.*

FINIS.

A Catalogue of ſome Books, Printed for Samuel Keble, *at the* Turks-Head *in* Fleet-ſtreet.

A Short View of the Immorality and Prophaneneſs of the *Engliſh Stage*: Together with the Senſe of Antiquity upon this Argument. By *Jeremy Collier*, M. A.

A Weeks Preparation towards a worthy receiving of the Lords Supper after the warning of the Church, for the Celebration of the Holy Communion; in Meditations and Prayers for Morning and Evening, for every Day in the Week. Alſo ſome Meditations to live well after the Receiving the *Holy Sacrament*.

The Church of *England Man's* private Devotions, being a Collection of Prayers out of the Common-Prayer-Book, for Morning, Noon and Night; and other ſpecial occaſions: By the Author of the Weeks preparation to the Sacrament.

The

The Holy-Days, or the Holy Feasts and Fasts, as they are observed in the Church of *England*, (throughout the Year) Explained: And the Reasons why they are yearly Celebrated. With Cuts before each Day.

Meditations upon living Holily, and dying Happily; with suitable Prayers at the end of each Chapter. Written by *Daniel Sennertus*, a Physician.

The Mourner Comforted: or Epistles Consolatory, writ by *Hugo Grotius*, to Monsieur *de Maurier*, the *French* Ambassador, at the *Hague*; perused and recommended to the World, by *John Scot*, D. D. in 12°.

Divine and Moral Discourses on divers Subjects, in 12°.

Epicteti Enchiridon: or the most Excellent Morals of *Epictetus*. Made *English* in a Poetical Paraphrase; by *Ellis Walker*, M. A.

The Historical Parts of the Old and New Testament in Verse, with one hundred and twenty Cuts, useful for Children, as well to invite them to the reading off, as to make them the sooner understand the Holy Scripture, in 12°. Price 2 *s*.

Rules for our more Devout Behaviour in the time of Divine Service, in the Church of *England*. Price 3 *d*.

An

An Explication of the Terms, Order and Usefulness of the Liturgy; or Common-Prayer of the Church of *England*, by way of Question and Answer, recommended to be learned after the Church Catechism.

A Table to all the Epistles and Gospels in the Book of Common-Prayer, so that you may find any Texts of Scripture; being contained in them. This Table may be put in your Common-Prayer Book.

Preparation to a Holy Life, or Devotions for Families and Private Persons; with directions suited to most particular Cases. Also Meditations, Prayers, and Rules for the more Pious observing the Holy time of *Lent*. By the Author of the Weeks Preparation to the Sacrament.

Death made Comfortable; or the way to Dye well. By *John Kettlewell.*

The Spiritual Combat, or the Christian Pilgrim: Translated from the *French*; Revised and recommended by Dr: *Lucas.*

The Degrees of Marriage, that which is ordered to be had in all Churches in *England.*

The worth of a Penny: or, a caution to keep Money: VVith the Causes of the Scarcity and Misery of the want

thereof

thereof: As alſo what honeſt Courſes Men in want may take to Live. By *Henry Peachman* M. A. Sometime of *Trinity* College, *Cambridge*.

Three Poems on St. *Paul's* Cathedral, *viz.* The Ruins. The Rebuilding. The Choire.

FINIS.

SOME
REMARKS
UPON
Mr. Collier's *Defence of his View of the* English *Stage,*

SOME

REMARKS

UPON

Mr. Collier's *Defence of his Short View of the* English *Stage*, &c.

IN

VINDICATION

OF

Mr. *Congreve*, &c.

In a Letter to a FRIEND.

LONDON:

Printed for A. Baldwin, near the *Oxford-Arms* in *Warwick-Lane*. 1698.

SOME
REMARKS
UPON
Mr. Collier's *Defence*, &c.

SIR,

I Receiv'd Yours, and with it Mr. *Collier*'s *Defence of his ſhort View.* I thank you for both, but cannot continue to do ſo, when you expreſs a deſire I ſhou'd give you my Opinion of that Book: You know I am naturally Lazy; and though I ſometimes make Remarks to pleaſe my ſelf, yet I hate taking the pains to put them in a Method fit for your Peruſal; therefore if you muſt be obey'd, you ſhall havet hem juſt as they are, Rough, Indigeſted, and about as Mannerly as the Defence which lies before me.

 First,

Firſt, For the Arrogancy of the Epiſtle to the Reader, where he calls all the Anſwerers of his dead-doing *Short View*, except Mr. *Congreve* and the Author of the *Relapſe*, Volunteers, which he proudly ſeems to imply are not worth his leaſt notice; they have yet enough upon their hands, they will find themſelves ſufficiently affected with the Fortune of their Friends; he looks upon them at preſent ſtunn'd by his mighty Arguments, but if ever they have the Courage to revive, he ſhall ſpeak with them hereafter: This is Magiſterial, and like Mr. *Collier*; yet ſincerely, for I have reſolv'd to give you my thoughts freely, conſidering the Leiſure the *Viewer* and *Reviewer* of Plays has, he might have found a Bone to pick even out of poor *Elkanah*'s; but he loves to read Plays better; and ſo much for that.

Next he has the ſatisfaction to ſee the Intereſt of Virtue not altogether ſunk; he is vain enough to believe he has ſhook the Stage, and hopes a total Overthrow will not be unacceptable: But I am inform'd, for all his mighty boaſting, and

the

the wondrous Progreſs he has made, the *Mourning Bride*, againſt which he rais'd his chief Battery, brought the greateſt Audience they have this Winter had: But all the World will not believe Mr. *Collier*'s Judgment infallible, no more than they will his Holineſs's. He goes on with a Catalogue of Smutty Plays, not exempting *Limberham*, which though forbid the Stage, finds a place in his Cloſet; and if the general Accuſation ſeems hard, he is ready to fall to Particulars; I believe him, and dare ſwear there's not a Line in any of the Comedies he has nam'd, that is bordering upon Smut, as the Modeſt Gentleman calls it, but has its Marginal Note, and can be produc'd with a wet finger.

Laſtly, he concludes almoſt in the very Words of one of Mr. *Dryden*'s Rants;

Take notice, Poets, you the Aggreſſors are.

Then he comes upon them with two dreadful We's, as if the whole Body of the Clergy were alarmed, and not only Players but all their Abettors were to be immediately excommunicated; when he might

might as well have ſaid, *Almighty I am blameable that I began no ſooner :* For upon Enquiry I do not find one Divine has thought it worth his while to neglect his graver Studies for the matter: Which I apprehend is a great Satisfaction to preſent Writers; for though they venture to diſpute with Mr. *Collier*, yet wou'd only in ſilence grieve, ſhou'd they be cenſured by that Church, which (Prophane as Mr. *Collier* eſteems them) I am apt to think they wou'd expoſe their Lives to preſerve.

One of the Anſwerers made an Obſervation worth remembring, *viz.* That the Stage fell, in our late Confuſions, with the Monarchy and Church; a certain ſign it was a Foe to neither; nay Mr. *Collier* amongſt his black Calumnies doth not charge it with promoting Rebellion; that Pious Work is left to the buſy Heads of Bigots and Enthuſiaſticks.

Thus far the Preface: But, my dear Friend, e're you proceed, I muſt beg you to recollect what I ſaid at firſt; not look upon this as a Regular Anſwer, or Defence of thoſe Gentlemen, who can do it it ſo much better for themſelves ; only the reſult of my preſent Thoughts, tranſmitted inſtantly to Paper, after my running over Mr. *Collier's* Book, and ſent to you without further Examination. Surely I ſhall have no occaſion to tell you how much I revere the Clergy ; you know my near Alliance, the particular Veneration I both owe and pay them ; yet I hope, without any Offence to thoſe good men which bleſs and adorn the Kingdom, I may charge Mr. *Collier* with Vanity, Uncharitableneſs, and Ill-nature.

If the Caſe is really ſo deſperate as he wou'd make it appear, methinks it ſhou'd be exploded more ſolemnly. When I ſee the Numerous Quotations he brings from Ancient and Modern Authors of Plays, I cannot help fancying he has ſpent too much time in the Studies he ſo bitterly condemns. If repreſenting Vicious Characters upon the Stage has occaſion'd the Practice of them in the Town, ſo his extracting the Faults only of all the late Plays he has meddled with, and haling them (as himſelf expreſſes on another occaſion) into his Book, has only ſerved to revive what elſe had paſſed perhaps utterly unheeded, or at leaſt not dwelt upon the Memory. I muſt confeſs my ſelf ſcandalized, when I hear Mr. *Collier* in one Line treating of the moſt Sacred Things our Religion contains, and in the next rallying or reflecting, as looſely as e're a Comick Poet of them all: This comes pretty near what he accuſes Lady *Plyant* with: And, by the way, that Sacred Name is too often uſed in Converſation upon the moſt frivolous occaſions; ſo that to put it indecently in the mouth of an ill Woman, ſhould rather deter than encourage the Audience to follow the Example.

Mr. *Collier*'s Reproofs to me ſeem inveterate; he writes with Animoſity, as if he had an Averſion to the Man as well as his Faults, and appears only pleas'd when he has found a Miſcarriage. Who, but Mr. *Collier*, wou'd have ranſack'd the *Mourning Bride*, to charge it with Smut and Prophaneneſs, when he might have ſate down with ſo many Scenes wherein even his malicious Chymiſtry cou'd have

have extracted neither? But against this Play, as if the Spirit of Contradiction were his delight, he musters all his Forces; and having passed Sentence as the Divine, commences Critick, and brings the Poetry to his severe Scrutiny, transcribes half Speeches, puts the beginning and end together, as in *Page* 92.

Drenched in briny Waves, pale and expiring,
Yet God-like even then.

His own charming Simile comes next, of a Seraphim and a drown'd Rat: So on the other Leaf he is got to the Image of Cats running up a Wall: Truly (*Frank*) I cannot but impute these abject Thoughts to his own reptile Mind; for I have read the *Mourning Bride* often, and it always inspired me with the noblest Ideas: Then he cavils at *Almeria*'s Answer, That she mourns for a Deliverance from the Wreck: This too is a Line taken out of a very probable and modest Reply. And here I conceive Mr. *Collier*, as indeed he has sometimes done before, seems to change his own Opinion;

 for

for I ſhou'd have thought he wou'd have liked *Almeria* better for commemorating her Deliverance in Mourning and Humiliation, than if ſhe had enjoined Mirth and Revelling, nay, perhaps Plays. Well, ſince Mr. *Collier* by his good-will ſhows nothing but what he thinks bad in the Play, pray give me leave to tranſcribe one Speech amongſt many, which ſure will ſtand Mr. *Collier*'s Teſt.

I've been too blame, and queſtion'd within piety
The Care of Heaven; not ſo my Father bore
More anxious Grief; this ſhou'd have better taught me
This Leſſon, in ſome hour of Inſpiration
By him ſet down, when his pure Thoughts were born
Like Fumes of Sacred Incenſe o're the Clouds,
And wafted thence on Angels Wings through Ways
Of Light to the bright Source of all. There in
The Book of Preſcience he beheld this Day,
And waking to the World and mortal Senſe,
Left this Example of his Reſignation;

This

This his last Legacy to me, which I
Will treasure here, more worth than Diadems,
Or all extended Rule of Regal Power.

Now I can pick Instruction and Delight out of this, and rest satisfied, if in a Tragedy the Passions rise either Love, Anger or Madness; I can behold them without one Thought of Imitation. It appears Mr. *Collier* has a very mean Opinion of the Capacity of the Audience, when he conceives all the Poets Flights will so far affect them as to practice the same; like *Don Quixote*, who cou'd not read Romances, but he must turn Knight-Errant. So several Characters in Comedy, which Mr. *Collier* has fell foul upon, I dare venture to affirm, the Poet never design'd for Examples; the fulsome *Belinda* in the *Old Batchellor* (as the cleanly-mouth'd Mr. *Collier* is pleas'd to call her) is shown full of Affectation; but I find it no where in the Play commended; and I always thought the Vanity was design'd to be exposed, not promoted; and if at last she's married to a Libertine she likes, where's the mighty Happiness? Doth not Fortune daily

daily produce the ſame in the World? Are not Fools, and Knaves, and Villains, often rich, and great, and in appearance happy? Yet this real Example doth not, I hope, tempt the good Man to forſake his Vertue for Preferment. What think ye now, dear *Frank*, of the Viewer? Do ye imagine he had any deſign to ingratiate himſelf with the ſeverer Clergy when he choſe this Subject, or to Cajole the Diſſenting Miniſters, when he took up their Quarrel, or make his Court yet higher? Since Plays are not in vogue, as they were the two laſt Reigns; truly I ſhrowdly ſuſpect he has a mind to tack about; he can change his Opinion, and be more complaiſant if he pleaſes; witneſs his ſoft Uſage of Mr. *Dryden*; in the Defence he ranks him amongſt the beſt Criticks; allows him a good Judge in Language, and mentions him, quite contrary to his Cuſtom, with much decency and reſpect; nay, I believe, ſhou'd the Old Gentleman become Poet Laureat again, Mr. *Collier* wou'd afford him a Panegyrick, notwithſtanding he tells the Author of the *Relapſe* he is not very full of them.

No,

No, there I think he is in the right, railing is properly his talent, and that he does with a guſt the Chriſtian Religion never inſpired; no plea of Youth, no acknowledgment appeaſes him; thus he makes himſelf a tinkling Cymbol, who whilſt he gingles with his Wit, and joins the Fathers and the Poets in his Citations, forgets the nobleſt gift of Heaven, *Charity*; proudly Judges and Condemns, finds Guilty or Abſolves by his own Authority.

Page 74. Kings he allows to be Diſciplin'd upon the Stage, but not the Church; ſurely 'tis a ſhame either ſhould be abuſed; but if a Tyrant, a Raviſher, a Blaſphemer, be extirpirated, and no good Prince is alarm'd at the matter, Why may not a good Prieſt ſee an ill one Charecteriſed, and not be concern'd, ſince even Mr. *Collier* and ten thouſand Inſtances allow, that failings are incident to them as well as to the reſt of human kind? Do but look over ſeveral *Spaniſh* and *Italian* Novels you have, and there you will find many abominable Stories of the Monks and Friars;

Friars; no Nations can be in greater ſubjection to their Ghoſtly Fathers than they, yet even with them the Bad are expoſed; all our Reformations and Amendments came from diſcovery of their Faults; nor can I think a Chaplain Ridiculed in ſuch a Family as Sir *Tunbelly's*, Reflects any more upon a ſenſible and learned Man in that Capacity, than Juſtice *Clodpate* in *Epſom-Wells*, does upon ſeveral Worthy Men that fill the Benches: That there are ſottiſh and unfitting Men amongſt the Clergy, muſt be granted, then why ſhou'd we not imagine ſuch a one in ſuch a Family; for ſure 'twou'd be the higheſt piece of rudeneſs to believe a Mr. *Collier* wou'd accept on't.

You ſee, Sir, I am as good as my word, jump from one thing to another, juſt as the hints I obſerved in reading occur, without minding which was firſt or laſt; and now I remember what the Biſhop of *Meaux* ſays, he calls *Iſrael* an innocent and undebauched People; when ſurely no Hiſtory extant ſets forth greater Villanies than the Sacred Story does of the *Iſraelites*, their

Abo-

Abominations were ſuch, that they were carried away Captive, and their Temple deſtroyed at laſt, for the completion of their Wickedneſs, notwithſtanding the ſtrongeſt Convictions, and their Prophets plain Prophecies, they Crucified the Lord of Life, and were afterwards driven from their beloved *Canaan*, with all the Cruelties Almighty Vengeance ever ſhow'd: Yet theſe People had no Theatres.

Page 89. Mr. *Collier* ſays 'tis much ſafer being of different Opinions, than agreeing in believing nothing. I grant him 'tis much better; a miſtaken Conſcience far above none at all; but for the ſafety he muſt excuſe me, ever ſince tender Conſciences produced Wars, and Murthers in cold Blood; ſince the beſt of Men and Kings, fell under the ſpecious Name of Conſcience: I ſhou'd not care for being Govern'd even by Mr. *Collier*'s Conſcience, he has too much fury in it for me; I never ſaw the Man, but his Writing makes my fancy repreſent him like one who had been heaving at a ſtately Fabrick, and miſſing there his aim, falls upon the next Cottage; like *Dionisius*, failing in State, sets upon the Stage, Born to be busy, and disturb whate're seems setled.

In another place he complains, *Manuel* is punished with Death for Tyranny, not Blasphemy; this certainly is trifling to the last degree; for if a Poet shows an Ill Man, and brings him to destruction, any reasonable Creature may put all his Faults together, and endeavour from the Moral to avoid them.

The 94th and 95th *Page* he imploys in ransacking the Poetry of the *Mourning Bride*; and since he can screw nothing there to Smutt and Profaneness, turns witty upon the Argument, and Burlesques about two Sides of Paper; yet for all what he has done, or threatens that he cou'd be larger, and this suffices only at present, as Mr. *Congreve* says, if the *Mourning Bride* is immodest, he is uncapable of Writing any thing modest: So I say, if that Tragedy is not allowable for its Decency, Morals and Poetry, I despair of ever seeing any thing of the Dramatick kind unexceptionable.

Page

Page 57. *Jeremy*'s Wickedneſs is again produced, and the Nice Mr. *Collier* is ſtrangely provoked, that the Varlet *Jeremy* ſhou'd talk of *Whoreſon appetites*. How this is Blaſpheming the Creation, to me appears flamingly ſurprizing; for I thought every Man, ſince the Fall of *Adam*, born with ſenſual and ſinful Appetites; therefore unleſs the word *Whoreſon* is Blaſphemy, I muſt acknowledge I cannot find it out.

The 47th *Page* he is buſy in Ridiculing Mr. *Congreve*'s Story of his Widow's Letter; and in the 55th gives a Sample of his Talent that way; for that *Vehiculum* underſtood Phyſick ſhou'd be taken in a Wheel-barrow, was never equall'd by all the Legends of the Wiſe-men of *Gotham*.

In troth *Frank* I am almoſt tired, tho' the fruitful Mr. *Collier* in every Page diſcovers Rancor, and a plain Deſire not to amend, but deſtroy.

This I obſerve in all Mr. *Collier*'s Remarks, there's an Air of Spite; for when he has pickt out any thing for his Cavilling purpose, if there's a following Line that will in the least extenuate, that's surely left out; nay, he will not allow of *Worthy's sudden Repentance*, but is so disappointed at it, that he gives poetick Rules for his continuing a Libertine to the end of the Play. I believe his chief Reason is, that he might have had further occasion for Correction. Then he is again displeas'd in the *Provok'd Wife*, that Sir *John Brute* is not punish'd enough. Truly, I think, his whole Character is one continued Punishment; and I wou'd no more chuse Sir *John's* Circumstances for the pleasure of his Libertinism, than I wou'd Mr. *Collier's* for the pleasure of Lashing on't.

One thing more, and I have done. In the 89th *Page*, he reflects upon poor Mr. *Lee's* Distraction; which shows the Temper of our Reformer, as much as if he had writ whole Volumes. Mr. *Lee* was the Son of an Eminent Divine; methinks that Consideration alone, since Mr. *Collier* sets up for the Champion of the Clergy, shou'd have deterr'd him from the Reflection: Besides, let him but look over the Records of *Bedlam*, and, as he

said,

ſaid, the good Women in *Homer* might Pole with the bad; ſo I dare ſay, the Miniſters under thoſe unfortunate Sufferings will far out-pole the Poets. Yet God forbid this ſhou'd be produc'd as an Argument either againſt our Religion or Paſtors, tho' Mr. *Collier* is, as he ſees, provok'd to uſe it for a Warning to poor Scriblers.

All my Acquaintance that diſcourſe this Matter, are convinced Mr. *Collier* has a particular Pique againſt Mr. *Congreve*; nay, ſome will go farther, and gueſs the Cauſe; perhaps there may be Lines of that Author's that vex the *Non-Juror* more than all the ſmutty Jeſts he has pickt up; Lines that Mourn the Royal *Paſtora*; Heroick Lines, that ſound the Glory of our Monarch. From this ſweet Poetry they judge his Gall is raiſed; which being gorged and full, overflows, nor ſpares the dead or living, Friends and Foes, the bitter Deluge reaches and beſpatters all.

Now I ſuppoſe, if Mr. *Collier* ſee this, he'd ask me if I thought his Gall contain'd as much as the Bay of *Biſcay*? Truly I believe his comes as near it as any

any Man's in the Three Kingdoms; however, I know you, dear Sir, have ſcarce enough to be angry with Mr. *Collier*: Therefore I ſhall ſay no more, but deſire you to excuſe the Faults and Length of this Epiſtle, which was occaſion'd by your own Commands. I am

Yours, &c.

FINIS.

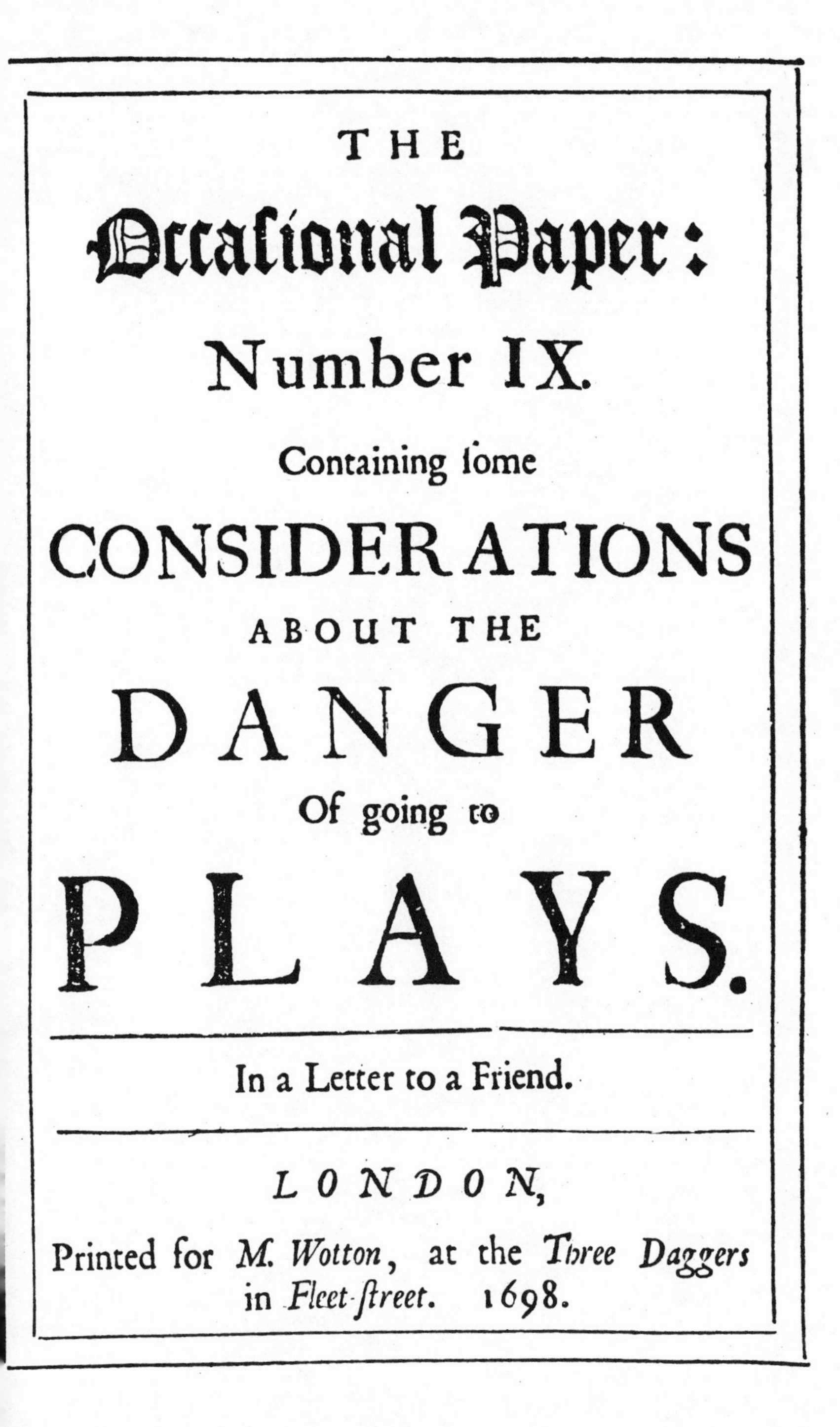

THE

Occasional Paper:

Number IX.

Containing some

CONSIDERATIONS

ABOUT THE

DANGER

Of going to

PLAYS.

In a Letter to a Friend.

LONDON,

Printed for *M. Wotton*, at the *Three Daggers* in *Fleet-street*. 1698.

THE

Occasional Paper:

Number IX.

Containing some

CONSIDERATIONS

ABOUT THE

Danger of going to Plays.

SIR,

BEing well assured that you sincerely desire to live as becomes a Christian, though you are not in Holy Orders; and that your complying with some things in use among those with whom you converse, is rather from a care to avoid being over-nice to the prejudice of Religion than

than any want of a due Concern for the Intereſt of it: I cannot refuſe the letting you ſee all at once, my thoughts of that, which having been at ſeveral times diſcourſed on between us, was never yet brought to a perfect Concluſion.

I have always found you doubting the *Lawfulneſs*, at leaſt the *Expedience* of going to *Plays*, *as they are now acted amongſt us*; and ſometimes you have ſeem'd to think it did not conſiſt with the Faith of the *Goſpel*, conſidering the Outrage committed there for the moſt part upon it, in one inſtance or other. And a freſh ſenſe of this I perceive has been given you, by the late *lively Account of the Stage*; the natural colours of which indeed are ſo black, as to be more than enough to affright thoſe who have any *Fear of Him that ought to be feared*, or any Dread of the Ruin of Men.

But for as much as the thread of that ſerious *Deſign*, may ſeem broken too often with Obſervations of Learning, and Reflections of Wit, to be cloſely follow'd by thoſe who are either not uſed to the one, or too fond of the other; the ſame good End may perhaps be helped forward a little, by ſetting this matter in a leſs interrupted Light, and a Simpler View.

And if things are as bad as they are there repreſented apart, looking on them together, you will ſcarce think thoſe expreſſions too hard, which in a more large and general State of the Caſe, you ſometimes thought did a little exceed. And very poſſibly the Zeal of ſome may have proceeded too far in running down to the ground, all *Diverſions of this kind* without any diſtinction: Tho' at the ſame time 'tis eaſie accounting for that ſeeming diſtance between thoſe

those who agree that *Vertue* shall be their common Design.

For they that are most for condemning these Entertainments, do not deny but some proper Instructions for civil Conduct at least, might thereby be gently instill'd; nor are they wholly against *Unbending* the Mind, as if they suppose the Spirits of Men wou'd carry them through the Business of Life without any Relief: But they think these, as they stand, are *dangerous Schools*: And, as for *Refreshment*, they see none in that which *unfits* us for our respective duties. And thus much is granted by those who wou'd shew a regard to the weakness of Nature, and not be over severe upon the Practice of those they think well enough of in other Respects.

Whenever you have inclined to favour these *Idle Amusements*, you have set them before you in an Innocent Dress, and contended for nothing but what might *Please* without giving *Offence*, you never design'd that what was *Prophane* or *Immodest*, should have your *Protection*; or to allow your self or your Friends a *Conversation* that was apt to *Corrupt*. You always hoped such *Spots* might be separated from those things you took in to *Divert*, and when you had made them as clear as you cou'd, you was easie to own, they might still be too freely indulged: For which reason I do not believe we shall differ much when we come to the End.

Taking then these *Plays* at the best, *pure* from all those *defiling Ingredients*, and *free* from the blemish of a *Vicious Resort*, a condition so perfect as we never yet saw the *Theater* in: All this would not make it a Place to be greatly frequented by those, that desire to keep their Minds in a suitable frame. No one wou d chuſe to converſe always with *Fiction* and *Show*, that cared to preſerve ſomething *Real* within ; Mens Minds in effect being nothing elſe but their uſual Thoughts, which paſſing continually through them with repeated delight, are ſure to leave their Image upon them ; as we can't but obſerve the *Admirers* of *Scenes* to have ſomething Romantick in all that they do.

Were we daily to be in the *Houſe* of *Feaſting* and the ſobereſt Mirth, our Spirits wou'd grow by degrees ſo frothy and light, that we ſhou'd not eaſily bring them to ſettle again on any thing that was worthy our care : Without ſomething now and then to raiſe them a little, they wou'd be dull and unactive, but *all* Relaxation wou'd make them too airy, and of no ſort of Uſe. They wou'd not ſerve to keep up our Souls from ſinking under the pleaſures of ſenſe, but ſo unawares betray us into them, by looſning the ſtrength we have to reſiſt, and improving the Charm, that tho' we ſuppoſed the whole Concern of the *Stage* to ſet out all Virtuous at firſt, we cou'd not expect its continuing long in that primitive State, before it run into ſome fooliſh Exceſs. For if Mens coming often and many together, on buſineſs, or kind and friendly Occaſions, is apt to lay a ſnare in their Way ; Nay if *Societies* form'd for the very promotion of Virtue , and ti'd to all the Diſcipline of it, are yet hardly kept from growing irregular : What can we hope from ſuch places of Concourſe, where Imagination expects to be rais'd, and the End is Delight ?

But I doubt we never began ſo fairly as this, becauſe our preſent *Corruption* is greater, than can well be conceiv'd to have ſprung from a *Root* that had at firſt no *Bitterneſs* in it.

Was

Was there nothing *ill* in the *Representations* themselves, yet there is so much of that by agreement of All, in the Vain *Behaviour of those that are there*; that they must needs be very fond of a *Play*, that can bring themselves to sit often and long in such *Company* for it.

And yet one woud think sufficient care had been taken by those on the *Stage*, to heighten and please the most vicious *Tast*. They appear to have study'd all the *Arts* of an easie *Defilement*, and to have left out no *Colours* that were likely to *Stain*. And that these may be sure to sink deep enough, their business is to discharge the Heart of all its pure and *native Impressions*, that it may be the better disposed to receive what *Tincture* they please.

Men must here begin to *unlearn* what their *Parents* and grave *Instructors* have told them in the very tenderest part of their care; and learn to suspect some of their first and plainest Notions of things. They are now to be taught how they might *Be*, without a Creator; and how, now they are, they may live best without any Dependance on his Providence. They are call'd to doubt of the *Existence* of *God*, or if that be allow'd them, 'tis only to question what *Notice* he takes: His Wise *Providence* at every turn is charged with *Neglect*, and often not for, that which has something of Precedent, supporting the Wicked; but which is *dreadfully New* disappointing their *Lusts*. Things they are no longer ashamed of, but publickly own, without so much as pretending to hide them from *God*, whom they are not afraid to treat as blind, or as giving *Consent*.

Thus

Thus is his *Holineſs* turn'd to the vileſt Reproach, his perfect *Knowledge* mention'd with ſcoffing, and his infinite *Power* deſpiſed.

Had we nothing to oppoſe to this, but that ſenſe of things which is natural to Us, and which even with all theſe Arts is not quickly defaced, we could not but ſtand amazed at ſuch Preſumptions as theſe, in ſo poor, and ignorant, and ſhort lived a Creature as *Man*; who came naked but lately out of the Earth, and muſt ſoon return to that condition again; who finds his ſight bounded in every thought, and meets with a thouſand ſtops in all his Deſigns; who every ſtep that he takes, wants ſome one to help him, and can ſcarce avoid being conſcious of that Hand to which he ows his Support. And yet as if it was honour to rave, this impotent Wretch muſt ſtill be daring at ſomething above him, as if he reckon'd it weakneſs to own of what he was made, and thought any ſubmiſſion too great a price to pay for being preſerv'd.

This cou'd not be accounted leſs than a Monſtrous *Extravagance*, had we no other *Rule* than that of *Reaſon* to meaſure it by; and a Man with only his ſenſes about him, would have a horrour to be thus Entertain'd. How then ſhall he that profeſſes the *Chriſtian Religion*, be able to bear ſo licentious a Treatment of all that is Good? a little degree of *temperate Zeal* wou'd turn him againſt ſuch *Abuſes* as theſe, and a middle proportion of *Faith* ſpread over the World, wou'd keep theſe Places from being ſo throng'd in their preſent State as they ſhamefully are.

They whoſe Dependence is on them, are ſo apprehenſive of this; that they are very induſtrious to weaken the force of that *Revelation* which darts it's

rays

rays so strongly against them, and discovers the vileness of that, they wou'd have Men admire. *Redeemer* and *Saviour* are Titles bestow'd upon infamous persons, which shews what sense they have of the want of him to whom they belong: And for what they are pleas'd to mention as *Sins*, they are sure to find as slight an *Attonement*. They make very bold with the *Grace* of God, and crave *Inspiration* to serve the ends of *Lust* and *Revenge*: In which that they may have nothing to check them, all *Flames* but their own are meer *Fancies* and *Dreams*; the sickly Thoughts of a future Account must be banish'd away, and *Conscience* dismissed as a weak and *Cowardly* thing.

That nothing may bind it, the Holy *Scripture* is used as a *Fable*, and at every turn brought out in disguise to be the better exposed: They will allow it to be but one of these two, either *Imposture* or *Madness*. And they who profess to make it their *Rule*, and to lead others by it, are scorn'd and traduc'd as running into *Frenzy* or *Cheat*, that no body else may have any regard to them or their way.

And when the *Fences* are thus broken down, what hopes can we have any *Virtue* shou'd stand without being impair'd at the least? Nor do they stick to pursue their design, but go on overturning the natures of things as fast as they can, and they have met but with too much Success.

The *Sense of God* being pretty well laid, the next thing to be sunk is all Respect to Superiours here; A *Prince* seldom appears to advantage, and 'tis easie to guess what use of this the Subjects will make. Imposing on *Parents*, and despising their Age is made a Mark of Spirit and Wit, and few are brought in *dull* enough to *Obey*. False Notions of *Honour* are here

C propo-

proposed as the ground of Esteem, and something of *Wildness* must go to the gaining *Applause*. To set up for themselves is the first thing young People must learn, and to think it brave to trample on all that stands in their Way: No *Greatness* like a thorough *Revenge*, nor any Spirit so *Mean* as that which *forgives*; *Abusing* those that honestly help them with their *Labour*, or *Goods*, has briskness and *Reach*, and a lively *Cheat* go's off with more *Reputation* than paying ones *Debts*.

Their *Friendships* are built upon serving their Pleasures; and so cannot but be as loose as that which holds them together: They who are Constant in breaking their *Vows*, shall here be caress'd as *Faithful* and *True*; but to shew *Fidelity* where it is ow'd, is too *formal* a business for those who have the *sense* to be *free*, and can relish nothing but what is forbid.

This makes them treat all *Regular Love* with that Stile of contempt, as if keeping of Measures was unbecoming our nature; and it was a shame to have the *Bed undefiled*. They mix with *Marriage* all the disagreeable things they can find to turn the *single* against it, and make those that are in weary and sick of so flouted a *State*: To increase their uneasiness under which Holy and Prudent Restraint, wandring Images are dressed up with all possible skill to affect them, and their heads are filled with the ways, of bringing these strange Desires to pass.

If this be the Case in the Main, as it plainly appears from the *Account* above mention'd, and might further be shewn by a very great addition of proof; then whether all this can be found at any one time, or whether some Days may not possibly be pretty clear of of it all but what is brought thither, is not very material, more than to determin, what particular *Plays* should always be chosen by those that will go to Any. For the fitness of allowing this Custom, or giving it any Encouragement, will not depend upon it's not being faulty alike in every Part; but 'tis enough to condemn it, if what has been said is the general Scope, tho' I doubt a Tryal wou'd shew that All offend in one thing or other.

Matters, then, being so, you will readily grant that they who go to be pleased, with any of those things which are hardly fit to be named; are wickedly bent, and live to the *Scandal* of that *Religion* they still make some shew to profess: Tho' not enough to give any hopes of their being reclaim'd, until we can find them perswaded indeed, that there is such a thing as *Sin* in the World, which will certainly have it's *Wages* at last.

But for those who are satisfied of this, and wou'd be loath to favour so much as the *Appearance of Evil*, they must be beg'd to consider, what *Vows* they are under, and *whereof they are made*, and How much Weaker still many *Others* may be, and What *Mankind* must come to in time if this *Humour* prevails, and How much the *next Life* must be at this rate more wretched than this!

Who that reflected what it was to *Renounce* the *World*, the *Flesh*, and the *Devil*, wou'd play with the sharpest Weapons of these, and offer themselves to such apparent *Danger* in *Sport*? there's not one of these *Enemies* but know how to take the utmost advantage, and will be sure to hit all the Blots that they give, they cannot without receiving some hurt, be so much as a Minute off from their *Guard*; and sure they do not come hither to *Watch*. Who

Who that had engaged to believe the *Christian Faith*, cou'd be content to see it exposed in every branch? To have their *Lord* and *Master* affronted for pretending to *Save*, and his *Ministers* scorn'd for the work he gave them to do! to hear a *Moment* preferr'd to the hopes of Eternity, and the *Judgment to come* thrown off with a Jest!

Who that had promised *Obedience* to God in all his Wise and Holy *Commands*, would bear the seeing them not only broken with ease, as often as Mens Inclinations rose up against them, but charged as unconcernedly too with harshness and folly! Their *Souls* one wou'd think shou'd be *vex'd* at such daring *Impieties*, and their *Spirits stirr'd* in them to see such Vices Adored; to find *Lewdness* vaunting it over Religion and Virtue, and usurping their place in a bold recommending it self to the affections of Men, with all those Advantages God design'd for the Adorning of Things that were really Good.

And who wou'd lightly endure all this, that from their Vows went on to reflect of what they were made? I suppose they wou'd find as they often complain, that they are Weak and Infirm, that while this *Flesh and Blood* is about them, their *Souls* are heavy, apt to decline, and seldom continue long in one posture and stay; that the World is upon them where ever they go, and the Devil busily marking their steps in every Path. That their *Faith* wavers upon many Surprises, their *Hopes* languish, and their *Fervour* decays; that in such cold seasons as these, their Spirits move but stiffly about, and seldom rise into any earnest petitions for Grace, but sink under the burden of *Prayer*, er, or steal away to some Trifle or other for a little Relief. That in such cases they have no *Heart* to go on with the rest of their Duties, all the Commandments of God growing grievous upon them, and *Repentance* beginning to have a discouraging face: That they know not how to follow their Master, wheresoever he goeth with all this Oppression, the *Cross* being now too much for them to take up and they feeling now no *Ease* in his *Yoke*.

And when they often find it thus to their grief, even where they think they take care to prevent it, wou'd one ever believe they shou'd act, as if they desir'd these Gloomy Returns, or thought the present Light they enjoy'd cou'd never be obscured again? How shall we do to think them sincere in their daily bewailings of *Human Infirmities*, while they continue to lay new weights on their Nature, as if the common Occasions of Life afforded not tryal enough for their faith, unless they call'd in *Temptations* to prove how much they cou'd bear?

Wou'd they that desired to be *fervent in Prayer*, and *attend* on the Lord with as little *Distraction* as their State would admit, fill their Heads with a crowd of extravagant thoughts, and run to see *Devotion* it self ridiculed, as if nothing was in it but Solemn *Pretences*? Or wou'd they that proposed to have their *Affections* in order, and their Appetites calm, chuse to thrust in themselves, where *Moving the Passions* is the business in hand, and such things are rendred inviting, to which the Heart is but too much inclined?

It cannot sure be safe for any to let *Errours* come often before them in such shapes, as may make them wish they were true. It must needs enfeeble their Minds, to have those Spirits divided that want to be fixed; and to converse with *loose Manners* brought down into fashion, and dress'd up with intent to deceive, is much too great a hazard to run in that little ground that is left to hope for the grace and assistance of God. where his *Spirit is griev'd*, and his *Being* deny'd.

And it is to be feared that they who come freest from any of that Pollution, which is in such quantities scattered there, have at least some dust to wipe off, before they get home: 'Tis hard staying so long in such a Cloud of black vapours and smoak, without having so much as a soiling remain; great odds it is, but something will stick for a sober reflection to banish, and a Prayer to correct. And who is there that wants more work of that nature than He has already.

But tho these shou'd be well enough armed to go away as clear as they came, yet Methinks they shou'd have some concern for the *Weakness of Others*, and the heat of their blood, as not to lead them into so *Contagious a Place*. All that go thither as yet uncorrupted, are not however so fully prepar'd, as to be above taking any Infection: Their Experience is little, and their Aversions to Evil but imperfectly settled; that it can't be expected they shou'd be proof against all the Assaults that are made in a pleasing Disguise. That *Root of Vanity* that secretly twists it self with their natures, is drawn out by degrees, and they are carryed on to the hopes of their *Liberty*, and of being *Admired*.

Now

Now were they to find no Company here, but such as were lost to good manners and shame, they wou'd suspect some deceit in the whole, and look well to themselves: But going under the shelter of many that have names for Religion, and I trust have it indeed; they are emboldned to think they are very secure, and that there is no need of being so Nice. Thus while those, by whose Example these are encouraged, preserve it may be themselves from the *Danger* they run; these unwary beholders take all that glisters for Gold, and are sadly betray'd.

St. *Pauls* advice to those that were strong, in another case is so fitted to this, that I cannot forbear the letting you have it at large. *Take heed* (says he) *least by any means this Liberty of yours become a Stumbling-block to them that are weak. For if any Man see thee which hast knowledge, sit at Meat in the Idols Temple, shall not the Conscience of him that is weak, be emboldned to eat those things that are offered to Idols? And through thy knowledge shall the weak Brother perish, for whom Christ dyed? But when ye sin so against the Brethren, and wound their weak Consciences, ye sin against Christ.*

Cor. 8, 9, 10, 11, 12.

And as forreign as this Instance may seem, was there any comfort in drawing the *Parallel*, we shou'd find but too great a Similitude between the *Places* in question, and the *Idolatrous Temples*; while the other difference that is in the case seems to lie on the side I am writing, that if Christians might sin in the use of their *Liberty* to the offence of their Brethren, much more wou'd they do so in such a Point as we have before us, where their own Consciences can hardly be clear, as we shall think it more difficult for them to be, if we consider yet further what *Mankind* will come to at last if this *Humour* prevails.

It

It is confess'd on all hands, that we live in a sad degenerate Age, and though some have suggested other causes of our horrid Declension, yet most considering People have the fairness to own, that the *Stage* has gon furthest in running us down to this low and almost Brutal condition; nor will there remain much question of this, if we can but agree what *Corruption* is.

If Exposing Religion with the Persons and things design'd for the keeping it up in the World, will pass for disorder; or if the Increase of Pride and Injustice, Blood and Revenge, are any signs of our being *Depraved*; or if want of Modesty, Obedience, and Love, contempt of Marriage, and neglect of it's Bonds may serve to shew the *foundations* of things to be at all *out of Course*. I think we have sufficient warrant to lay the confusion at that *Door*, which opens to these.

That these things are taught there, and found in the World, can be no way deny'd, and then it is not of any great use to enquire, whether strictly speaking they were at first brought from thence, or carryed thither. For when our Bodies and Minds are much out of order at once, 'tis hard saying where the Distemper began; and the less material to know, when both must have their Cures apply'd, and it is to the advantage of neither, that they go on to hurt one another. If the ill humour does not begin in the place we suppose, it is there at least increased to a head, and thrown out again into all parts of the body, many of which to be sure first have it from thence, tho' they afterwards help to keep up the Spring: And if this pestilent Matter, be not only thus suffered to circulate, but assisted to spread, the *Sickness* will quickly be *unto Death*.

For

For whatever some fancy, a Nation can never live long without any Religion, nor Religion subsist without some to attend it as their principal Care: So that shou'd it indeed come to pass, that no body minded what Men of this Character said, as these *Teachers* would have it, Darkness with all it's hideous works wou'd soon cover the face of the Land, and make it fit for the Stroke.

We are already almost advanced to the brink of the Pit, by People's unlearning only what once they were taught, of the Honour and Advantage of *Marriage*, and the mutual Duties of Husbands and Wives, which are indeed so grosly forgot, that the Offenders have well nigh made their own Doctrine against it, appear to be true: But then it cannot confute it self better, then by bidding so fair to destroy all the Comfort and Use of a *Social Life*: For if Mankind cannot indeed be happy in Wedlock, they are in a very deplorable State.

It was deservedly thought a Monstrous Error in those that declaimed against Marriage of old, as bringing more Creatures into the World to Sin, and be punished for it; tho' Salvation and Purity were their design: How much then above these are they to be blamed, who wou'd fain bring it into discredit, without any intent to keep Souls from Miscarrying, or set an unspotted life in it's place; but on purpose to spread their *Abominations* the wider, in defiance of all the Threatnings of God denounced against them, and those they defile.

And who then that had any serious concern for the Glory of God, or the welfare of Men in this life or the next, wou'd not stop and consider a while with themselves, how far they shou'd give any countenance to ſuch *Recreations*, as tend to diſturb even the beſt of their preſent Enjoyments and Peace, and lead to extreme *Deſpair* in the *End*? For however Men may with vain words be ſadly deceived, *the Wrath of God cometh upon the Children of Diſobedience, becauſe of theſe things*, and when they have mock'd all they can, they will find that He is *a Conſuming fire*.

Compaſſion, then, one wou'd think, ſhou'd work upon thoſe that are good, to diſcourage by all their Endeavours, ſuch Cuſtoms as bring on the ruine of many, and do hurt to the whole, tho' they ſhou'd have ſtrength to go in, without being tainted themſelves: Not that they can pretend to be ſafe even from taking *Infection*, if once their *Preſervatives* come to be frequently uſed, and to loſe their Virtue, as they will by degrees. At leaſt they will want a great deal of fulfilling the duty incumbent upon them to *Adorn their Holy Profeſſion*, and can hardly aſſure themſelves of their being redeemed from the vain Converſation they had in the World. Thoſe allowances to this, at beſt, *careleſs ſpending of time*, which a little ſhare in it, will bring them to make, cannot chuſe but abate a great part of their *Zeal*, and ſlacken their pace in their ſpiritual Courſe; to which theſe *Entertainments* are ſo flat a Reverſe, that *Dying daily*, and going to them, ſet out as they are, can ſcarce have their good Opinion together.

And who then that deſired to perfect their natures, by a patient *ſtriving for Maſtery* over their Luſts, and following the *Captain* of their *common Salvation* thro' all the Paths of an humble Obedience, wou'd care to appear under ſo different a *Banner*, and encumber their Souls with more than they need, of what muſt again be thrown out of their way, or hinder their winning the *Prize*.

This

This being the caſe, good Chriſtians certainly cannot have the much eaſier thoughts of ſuch freedoms as theſe, for not finding them in ſo many words expreſly forbid. Such as theſe will conſider the end and deſign of the Goſpel, and the frailty of Man, and think themſelves obliged to be jealous of any faſhion that tends to increaſe the weakneſs of one, and leſſen the force of the other: When this plainly appears to be the Conſequence of any Indulgence, they allow it to lay as full a Reſtraint, as cou'd be ſet by one or two particular Texts, which a corrupt underſtanding wou'd be at leſs pains to evade.

And yet if it blemiſhes any opinion to be Earthly and Senſual, or if *Evil Communications* are ever the worſe for their effect upon *Manners*: If to cheriſh a *Mind that is at Enmity with God*, and declared to be *Death*, be oppoſing his Will, and endangering the Souls of them that ſupport the Reſiſtance; Accuſations abound againſt the Cuſtom that paſſes for ſo inoffenſive a thing.

If *caſting down Imaginations, and every high thing that exalteth it ſelf againſt the knowledge of God, and bringing into Captivity every thought to the Obedience of Chriſt*, be the Warfare of thoſe that wou'd go by his Name; If arming themſelves againſt the *Luſt of the Fleſh, the Luſt of the Eye, and the pride of Life*, be that Task he has ſet them to do; If a *chaſt Converſation coupled with fear*, and *letting their Light ſo ſhine before Men*, that they may ſee 'em *do all to the glory of God*, be the duty of Chriſtians; we have places enough to ſhew them of what importance it is, to withdraw from thoſe that walk ſo very diſorderly, as wou'd not have been in the times of a

livelier

livelier Faith, allow'd the outward Communion of Saints.

Nor is the Case so mightily altered from what it was then, unless it be for the worse; as that we shou'd from thinking them wholly unworthy to come into our *Assemblies*, run flocking to theirs: For what vileness has ever offended the World, which is not exceeded if possible there? Can the Burlesquing an absurd Religion, or Mocking it upon the Stage be so bad as defying one that is reasonable and wise, or paying Honour to *Gods that were not*, be like the blaspheming him that is *True*? This cannot sure in reason be thought, whatever Excuses People may find to palliate that which they cannot find in their Hearts to condemn.

Nor is that primitive Spirit so wholly extinct, but that some in our days, and of *that Religion* which carries more marks of the World, then God be thanked are met with in ours, have dared to appear directly against that vain Practice, which notwithstanding sits easie on many of so much a *stricter Communion* than theirs. And this Instance is so far from being the worse for coming from *France*, that it is a great deal the more fit to be urged in the present debate. For if, in a Country disposed to a *lighter Temper and Air*, where the *Church* has greater Corruption, and the *Theater* fewer, there can yet be whole Bodies of *Casuists* found, disallowing the sight of their *Modester Plays*; Methinks it shou'd not be thought an Absurdity here, to go about to disswade so *thoughtful* a *People* as we reckon our selves, from going to ours which shew so little of that Reformation to which we pretend.

And

And least this should seem to be only the sense of some retired *Divines*, I beg leave to observe that the same censure is also pass'd by a *Prince of the Blood*, as highly Esteem'd for his *Learning* as *Birth*. And I wish his Example were follow'd here, that the shameful *Indignities* put upon Persons of the *Highest Descent* by those of the *Meanest*, wou'd stir up some excellent Spirit of that Eminent Rank, to shew them how much beneath them it was, to stoop so low to be thus coarsly entertained: And that it betray'd a want of *Honour* as well as *Religion*, tamely to see themselves as well as their *Maker* abused, and to seem pleased with that in a Croud, which said or done before them any where else, they wou'd be obliged to resent as the highest Affront.

P. of Conde. *Vid. traite de la Comedie.*

At least I hope that one way or other, they will be convinced how much it concerns them to put a stop to this Insolent Course, and find out some other *Diversions*, till these at least are reform'd, more suitable to the Christian Religion, and less threatning their Virtue and Fame. And such no doubt may be found, tho' some perhaps will be apt to reply, that, at this way of talking, all are condemn'd.

But this I conceive is not fair, nor rightly deduced from what has been said; good reasons I know are sometimes press'd with these kind of Extremities, when Men have not a mind to admit their natural force; and to hinder inferring any thing from them, they frowardly insist on their proving too much: And thus I think it wou'd be in those, who shou'd offer to urge that this sort of arguing puts an end to all kind of Mirth.

For are then all Diversions alike? And can there be none without such follies, as no Man in his sense wou'd endure? Must all easie Conversation be lost, unless Men

F

have

have leave to be looſe and profane? And can there be no coming together of Strangers or Friends, but ſome naked Vice muſt dance and be praiſed, or ſome Virtue made a Sacrifice of, to fill up the Feaſt?

There may very well be, and no doubt but there is, in moſt Converſation, a great deal of that which ſhou'd never be there; and this is what one cannot wholly avoid without leaving the World. But can this be reaſon why we muſt let People make to themſelves new and needleſs Occaſions of Vanity, and lay dangerous ſnares in the way of unwary People? I ſhou'd rather think the Argument lay; that ſince there were ſo many faults, in all parts of the World and divertion of life, Men ſhou'd not look out for more of this Traſh to offend their Company with, and foment the Diſeaſe, but get clear away from all the Infection they cou'd, and lay in a Stock of ſuch agreeable and wholſom proviſions, as might enable them to treat others with Safety and Eaſe, and ſometimes to correct the ill humours they found.

But then they muſt not go to ſuch *Books* and preſcriptions for theſe, as are full of the leaven they ſhou'd put out from amongſt them, and can ſerve for nothing elſe but to poyſon their Food: To converſe with Impiety here, is to give it all the advantage they can, it is to ſurrender the Mind entirely up to whatever aſſaults it, without being able to ſave ſo much as a ſtragling thought. For they whoſe *Cloſets* are fill'd with nothing but theſe, do not even pretend to reſiſt the force they call in, and a good Book ſtanding odly by, will be little ſecurity, againſt the ſtrong Deluſions of thoſe they read with content: And therefore they who wou'd have their

own

own virtue preſerved, and ſee more in the World, muſt not only avoid ill commerce abroad, but reject it at home, and employ their Retirements in preparing themſelves to appear in publick without danger, and to ſome kind of Uſe.

This care, I am ſure, of our ſelves, and this Compaſſion one of another, God and Nature and the Goſpel require; and how much or how little ſoever others may be affected at this, you Sir, I dare ſay, will think beſt of your ſelf, when you tread moſt in the ſteps of your *Saviour*, and like him, *go about doing good*: When you relieve the Afflicted, aſſiſt your Neighbours, and comfort your Friends; when you pleaſe and benefit thoſe that deſire to hear you, and Reverence and Kindneſs and Truth, are the Law of your Tongue. When a meek and quiet Spirit adorns you, and Piety gives the grace to your looks, when your Religious Example ſhines ſo lovely and clear, as to draw thoſe after you, to whom it ſhews the beautiful way; and Vanity has not the face to appear; then, and not much before then, will you think you have made ſome Advance to Peace and a Crown.

In hopes of that deſired Succeſs,

I am,

SIR,

Your, &c.

FINIS.

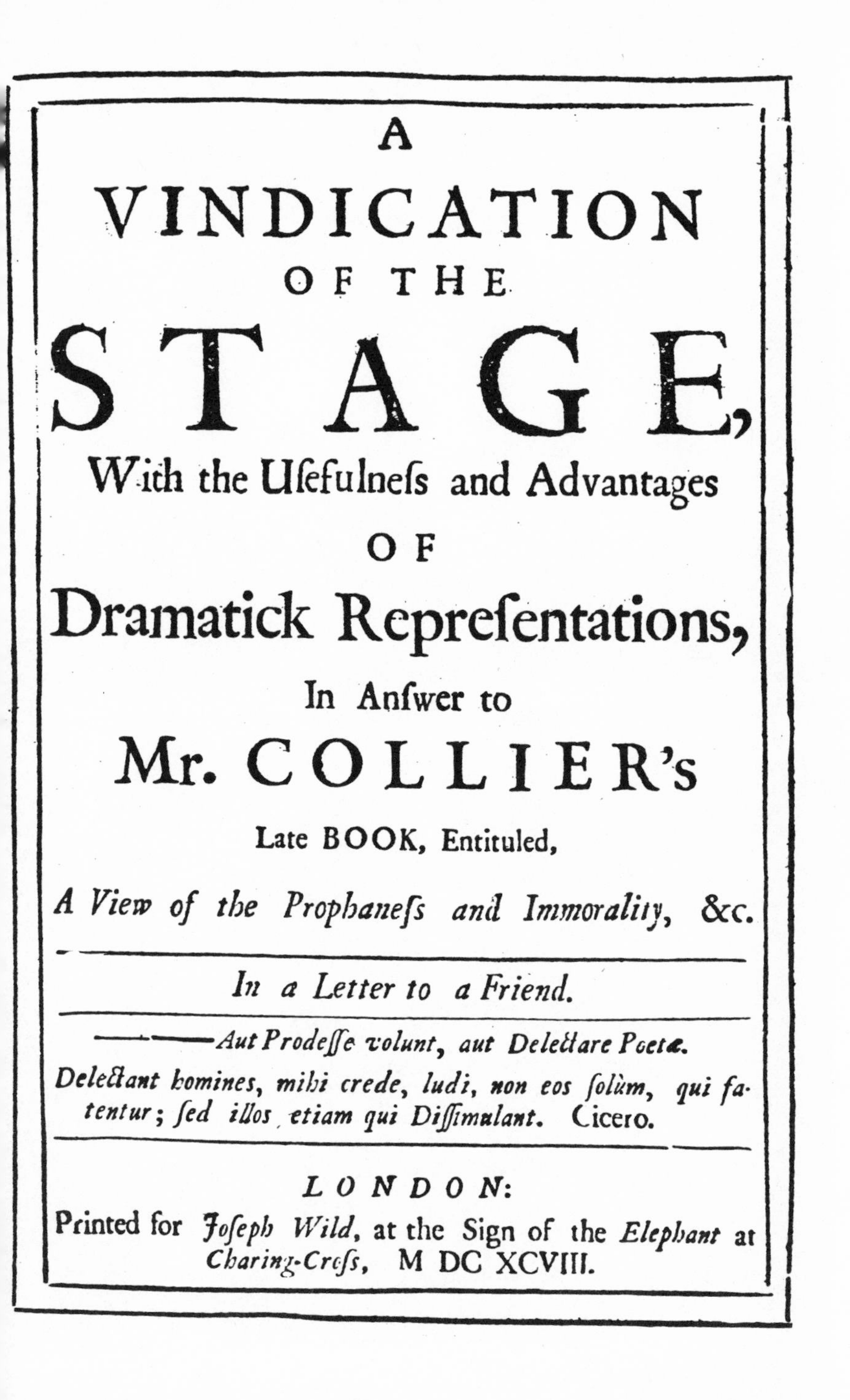

A

VINDICATION

OF THE

STAGE,

With the Uſefulneſs and Advantages

OF

Dramatick Repreſentations,

In Anſwer to

Mr. COLLIER's

Late BOOK, Entituled,

A View of the Prophaneſs and Immorality, &c.

In a Letter to a Friend.

——*Aut Prodeſſe volunt, aut Delectare Poetæ.*

Delectant homines, mihi crede, ludi, non eos ſolùm, qui fatentur; ſed illos etiam qui Diſſimulant. Cicero.

LONDON:

Printed for *Joſeph Wild*, at the Sign of the *Elephant* at *Charing-Croſs*, M DC XCVIII.

A VINDICATION Of the STAGE, &c.

SIR,

I Return you my thanks for the Present you sent me of Mr. *Collier*'s Book against the Stage, you cou'd indeed have thought of nothing wou'd have pleas'd me better; it made a mighty Noise with us in *Staffordshire*, his Arguments were cry'd up as Invincible, and all the precise old Folks here (who perhaps had never seen a Play in their lives) join'd in a loud Out-cry against the wicked Stage: To shew you my Gratitude, and to encourage you still to remember your Friend at this distance, I have sent you some Thoughts as they occurr'd on a slight perusal of it; for let the old Maxim be never so common in our Mouths, *viz. Vertue is its own Reward*; yet we always find, where it meets with no other, it is very apt to die and wither, like a Plant in a dry Soil it is seldom seen gay and flourishing without the assistance of some kind and refreshing Showers; and I believe we need go no farther for an Instance of this Nature, than to Mr. *Collier* himself, for I am strangely apt to fancy that the *Fifty Pounds* had a greater influence with him, than the stab

 he

he suppos'd he shou'd give to Vice and Debauchery; this however I must confess a course Complement, but you know my free humour, and have reason to except your self out of the general Rule. If I stay longer here, I may send you these Thoughts better digested, or some farther Remarks on the same Author.

Mr. *Collier* has employ'd abundance of Rhetorick in his Cause, he has made use of all his Judgment in digesting his Matter, and shew'd his great Reading in his Quotations from the Greek and Latine Poets, and the Ancient Fathers; with great skill in the choice of his Arguments, and given them so bright and dazling a lustre, that it is no wonder if many heedless and unobserving Readers are carried over to embrace his Party: But I think there is not really that strength in them as is fancied, which I shall endeavour, as well as I can, to show, under the disadvantage of but an indifferent Memory, and the want of all manner of assistance from Books; nay, I cannot so much as procure those Plays he so severely condemns.

In his Introduction he tells us, *The business of the Stage is to recommend Vertue, and discourage Vice.* Now whether or no Plays (Comedies I mean) have any business at all, or whether their chief and prime business is not to dievert the Audience, and relieve the Mind fatiegu'd with the business of the foregoing part of the day, is yet a disputable point: Nor shall I easily grant his Proposition. For my part, when I go to the Theatres, it is with this intention alone, *viz.* to unbend my Thoughts from all manner of business, and by this Relaxation to raise again my wearied Spirits, and fit them for the Affairs of the next day; the Mirth and Jollity of the place, like a well prescrib'd Cordial, performs its Operation, enlivens my drooping Thoughts, and passes clearly off, working a pleasing Cure, and leaving no impression behind it. This is my Opinion of Comedy, and not only mine,

but

but alſo of ſeveral very Famous and Learned Perſons; however there are but few of our Comedies that will not afford ſome Moral Inſtructions too; and our Tragedies may ſtand the teſt, even by his Rule, with any of the Ancients.

His chief Objections againſt our Plays are, That they are Immodeſt, Prophane, and Immoral; and that the Sacred Order of the Clergy is abus'd and ill treated; I ſhall endeavour to ſay ſomething on each of theſe Heads.

Firſt, He tells us they are Immodeſt, and generally Smutty. I ſhall give him an anſwer from the Celebrated Sir *Philip Sidney, Comedy* (faith he) *is an Imitation of the Common Errors of Life; now as in Geometry the Oblique muſt be known, as well as the Right; and in Arithmetick the Odd as well as the Even, ſo in the Actions of our Life who ſeeth not the filthineſs of Evil, wanteth a great Foil to perceive the Beauty of Virtue; and little Reaſon hath any Man to ſay that men learn the Evil by ſeeing it ſo ſet out, ſince there is no Man living, but by the force Truth hath in Nature, no ſooner ſeeth theſe Men play their Parts but he wiſheth them in* Priſtinum. And *Cicero* tells us, *Comedia eſt Imitatio vitæ*, where every one might ſee himſelf hit in ſome part or other. So that I know not how they can avoid giving Deſcriptions of Debauchery, till the World has left the Practiſe of it; when Men no longer Swear, you will hear no Oaths in the Play-houſe, and ſo of all other Vices. Beſides, if Delight be the end of Comedy, the Charge will fall on the People, and not on the Poets, ſo that at leaſt Mr. *Collier* has laid his Arguments wrong, for if the Spectators were diſpleas'd with the Repreſentation, the Poets wou'd quickly change it. This, granting his Charge were true, but Mr. *Collier* perhaps may fancy a bad meaning where there is none, this heavy Condemnation may be only a Bugbear of his own raiſing, to fright away the faireſt and beſt Part of the Audience, I mean the Ladies. How has it happen'd that he has made

ſuch

ſuch Diſcoveries ? When others, as clear-ſighted as himſelf, nay, and as modeſt too, never found any ſuch faults. Further, his dwelling ſo long on the Subject of Debauchery, argues ſomething of Delight and Pleaſure in the Caſe. It puts me in mind of a Cuſtom common among the Native *Iriſh*, which is, that they cannot endure to go dry in their Feet, but when they Travel, run into every Puddle they find, and are very angry, if for want of a Bog or Ditch they are forc'd to be cleanly, tho' ne'er ſo ſhort a time. Mr. *Collier* may apply the Story at his leiſure.

And here I can't but think the Ladies have great cauſe to thank him for his kind Inſtructions; they, harmleſs Innocents, found nothing amiſs before, but Mr. *Collier* has taken care they ſhall not be ſo ignorant hereafter; for he, in his great Wiſdom, has pointed out the places, where he promiſes they may be furniſhed with Smut in abundance.

His way of Complementing them on this account, is ſomething odd; but that's not to be regarded in him. He well knows, that ſeveral of thoſe Plays he Condemns, are immediately Dedicated to Ladies of the Higheſt Quality, and almoſt all of them have gain'd the Approbation of the Fair Sex: Now, by his pretending to find theſe faults of Smuttineſs and Obſcenity, he very boldly aſſerts, that they encourage and are pleas'd with the Crimes; this every one muſt own is very Obliging, Civil, and Well-bred.

But perhaps, to excuſe himſelf he will ſay, that the Ladies did not obſerve any ill in what they encourag'd, and that if they had, they wou'd have ſhew'd their diſlike of it. But this he ſhall anſwer himſelf in Page 11. where ſpeaking of Womens Modeſty, he tells us, *It is wrought in the Mechaniſm of their Bodies, that intuitive Knowledge ſcarce makes a quicker Impreſſion: And that the Enemy no ſooner approaches, but the Blood riſes in oppoſition, and looks Defiance to an Indecency.* So that if there had been the Enemy which

he

he pretends, the Ladies wou'd have ſound it out without his interpoſing in the buſineſs, and if there was no Enemy, we muſt imagine him a little Ally'd to *Quixotiſm*, or troubled with ſomething like a Wind Mill in his Brains, that for the ſake of Quarrelling only, he will Combat with the Air. But the Ladies have not found this Enemy, therefore we muſt think his needleſs Aſſiſtance Impertinence, and his Charge vain and frivolous: He was willing however to ſhow his Skill and Dexterity in the vile Employment of raking among Filth and Dirt. Further, it is an unlucky Blot to his Prudence, in diſturbing and bringing to light what was ſo well hid before, when he himſelf ſeems aware of the dangerous Conſequences it may produce if it wore a *Diſguiſe*, as he ſays Page 4th, he was very much to blame for taking it off. You ſhall have his own Words Page 5. *For ſuch a Liberty may probably raiſe thoſe Paſſions, which can neither be diſcharg'd without Trouble, nor ſatisfi'd without a Crime; 'tis not ſafe for a Man to truſt his Vertue too far, for fear it ſhould give him the ſlip.* It ſeems he did not take his own Advice in this particular: For, we find he truſted his Vertue very far, tho' not too far I hope, for fear of the worſt. In Page 7. he tells us, *it is almoſt a fault for them* (meaning the Fair Sex) *to underſtand they are ill us'd*; I wou'd ask Mr. *Collier* if he then doth not commit a fault too, who ſhews them they are ill us'd? Nay, perhaps wou'd engage them into a belief they are ill us'd, when they are not? Thus much for the Moderns.

Now he proceeds to quote all the exceptionable places under this Head, that are to be found among the Ancients; but, by his favour, there are ſeveral other places may be produc'd, which he has either forgot or skip'd over; I ſhall inſtance in two only at preſent; one Example of this kind ſhall be the Scenes betwixt the *Nurſe* and *Phedra* in *Euripides*, and there I think we may meet with as home ſtrokes

of

of Obſcenity, and as pithy arguing on the Subject, as can be found among the Moderns, It will be but a lame excuſe, to ſay it is the *Nurſe*, and not *Phedra* the Lady, ſpeaks the faulty Sentences, for if the Audience have them, the matter is not much by whom they are convey'd: They will make as deep an Impreſſion, and find as ready Entertainment from the *Nurſe* (who by the way was rather her Companion and Confident) as from *Phedra* her ſelf.

The other ſhall be from the *Phedra* of *Seneca*, and here we find the Lady her ſelf openly owning and juſtifying her Inceſtuous Love, and the *Nurſe* adviſing the contrary; nay, we have both *Lady* and *Nurſe* praying to the Gods to aſſiſt in the wicked deſign on her Son-in-law, and uſing all imaginable means to bring the buſineſs about; the *Nurſe* falls briskly upon him, tells him a City-Life with Women is very comfortable and delightful; but he is deaf to the Charm, profeſſes a mortal hatred for Women, and expreſſes his Love to range the Country Plains; *Phedra* falls in to the Conference, and Swounds at his Indifference, but being taken up in his Arms, ſhe recovers, and argues very hotly and ſhamefully for her Paſſion; but the Youth ſtill reſiſting, ſhe will needs Raviſh him; (*Etiam in Amplexus ruit*) all this is openly ſhew'd on the Stage. I defie Mr. *Collier* to produce me one ſuch Obſcene Inſtance in all our *Engliſh* Plays.

It will not be much amiſs neither to put Mr. *Collier* in mind of the *Ludi Florales*, which were Anually Celebrated among the *Romans*, for tho' they were not Stage-Plays, yet they will ſerve to ſhow that we are, contrary to his Opinion, ſomething Modeſter than they. They owed their Original to a Famous Whore, who having got an Eſtate by her Trade, left the Commonwealth her Heir, on this Conditiou, That every Year they ſhou'd Celebrate her Birth-day with Publick Sports; and the Solemnity conſiſted in a Company of Lewd Strumpets, that ran about the City naked, Singing,

Dancing, and uſing the moſt Obſcene and Laſcivious Poſtures: And this was done by Publick Order and Command. This I think is ſufficient to let us ſee, that contrary to Mr. *Collier's* Opinion, the Ancients were as Immodeſt and Obſcene as the Moderns, if not worſe: But we will look into his Book, to ſee if he does not contradict himſelf in the Matter.

And indeed I cannot forbear ſmiling, to ſee this Gentleman take ſuch Labour and Pains in three or four whole Pages, to prove that the Ancient Poets were not guilty of this Crime of Smuttineſs and Obſcenity; when but a little before in Page 5. he told us, *it was for this very Reaſon that* Plato *baniſh'd Poets his Commonwealth.* Now I hope Mr. *Collier* will not be ſo very hardy as to ſay, That *Plato's* Acquaintance lay among the Moderns. This was a very unlucky Sentence, and his forgetting it, is a great proof of the old Proverb, *Great Wits have ſhort Memories.* And ſince we have occaſionally mention'd *Plato*, it will not be wholly impertinent to let you ſee that honeſt *Plato* himſelf, tho' one of their Grave Philoſophers, writ Verſes more Lewd and Scandalous, than the very worſt that can be found among our Poets. They were writ on the Kiſſing of *Agatho*, and done from the *Greek* by *Decimus Laberius.*

Dum Semihulco Savio,
Meumq; Puellum Savior
Dulcemq; Florem Spiritus,
Duco ex aperto tramite:
Anima tunc Ægra & ſaucia,
Cucurrit ad Labia Mihi;

Rictumq; in ore pervium,
Et Labra pueri Mollia
Rimati itineri Transitus;
Ut Transiliret Nititur.
Tum si, moræ quid plusculæ;
Fuisset in Coitu Ostula
Amoris Igni percita;
Transisset, & me linqueret.
Et mira prorsum res foret,
Ut ad me fierem Mortuus
Ad puerum ut intus viverem.

And if a Bearded Philosopher, that pretended to a remarkable Strictness and Severity of Life, writ so Lewd and Loosely, we may well imagine their Poets were not behind hand in the Matter.

Well, but he tells us Page 5. *That we may take notice the Ancients had no Smutty Songs in their Plays.* This I must confess is an extraordinary Observation, but I am afraid it will slip away from him before he is aware: I wou'd fain know what grounds he has for it; is it because he finds none Printed with their Plays? Now I will offer this in Answer, that it is very likely the *Dramatick Poet* never meddled with the Musical Entertainment, but that either the Masters of Musick were so much Poets as to make their own Words, or some other of an Inferior Class were hired to the purpose; and it is very probable, that the *Musick* and the *Dramma* were reckon'd so different, that the *Drammatick Writer* thought himself

himself not oblig'd to take any care of it; and this perhaps may be the best Reason can be given; why we find none of their Musical Entertainments among the *Latin Comedies*, after the *Chorus* was expell'd the Stage: But this is not all neither, we have, I fancy, all the Reason in the World, to believe they rather went beyond us in this particlular; for we are sure, and Mr. *Collier* himself confesses it, that the *Pantomimi*, the *Gestures* and *Dancing* were extreamly Lewd and Scandalous; and that their Musick must be conformable to the Occasion, none I believe will doubt, nor do I think we have any great Reason to question that they wanted Vocal Musick to joyn with the Instrumental. Thus have I done, what my haste, and the disadvantages I labour under, will permit on this Head; and I think have sufficiently prov'd that the Ancients were as Smutty and Obscene as any of the Moderns can be; not but that I own there are some things however might be regulated on the *English* Stage, and I wish with all my Heart all Indecencies were remov'd, for there cannot be a more Effectual and Noble Method of instructing us, than by *Drammatick Representation*; but of this more hereafter. I shall pass to his next Charge, that of Prophaness.

And under this Head, he Charges them with using Oaths in their Plays, yet produces no Instances to prove his Assertion; therefore we may very well conclude it false and frivolous, for had it been true, his Wit or his Malice had found it out; and he, who has taken all manner of advantages against them upon all accounts, and has rais'd Mountains out of every Mole-hill, wou'd never have over-look'd such an opportunity of Triumph.

Mr. *Collier* was very hardly diſtreſs'd to make good this Charge, ſince he was forc'd to complain of a Word, becauſe it happen'd to have two Letters that do indeed belong to an Oath, but perhaps this Gentleman's Averſion to Oaths is ſo very great, that the ſight of the Word ſcar'd him; and ſo without further conſideration he condemn'd it. Averſions often cauſe very unaccountable Effects. I remember a Story of Sir *William Temple's*, of one, *Who in his Youth being very cloſely purſued by a Madman, had but juſt time to ſhut the Door of a Houſe he ran into, before his Purſuer was at it; and the Impreſſion ſtuck ſo faſt upon him ever after, that when he was a Man, he never enter'd a Door but with fear on his Spirits, and cou'd not forbear turning his Head back as he enter'd.* This Squeamiſh Gentleman perhaps has had ſome ſuch terrible Fright, which he can never wear off. One Comfort is, if Oaths do happen in his way, he very well knows how to refuſe them.

But perhaps in ſome very few places an Oath may be met with, and it may be neceſſary too, for I deſire Mr. *Collier* to ſhew us how a *Libertine*, a *Debauchee*, can be repreſented, but by making him act and ſpeak accordingly.

It is *Horace's* Rule,

Sit Medea ferox invictaq; flebilis Ino;
Perfidus Ixion, Io vaga, Triſtis Oreſtes.

Every one muſt be repreſented as they are: He may as well complain of a Painter for drawing an ugly Face like, as of a Poet for making a Wicked Perſon Swear and talk Lewdly, a Looſe Behaviour is as Eſſential to de-

ſcribe

ſcribe the one, as a Bad Complexion and Irregular Features are to delineate the other.

It is very obſervable, that upon this Head, he has not endeavour'd any Parrallel betwixt the Ancients and the Moderns; he cannot but very well know it wou'd have been extreamly to his diſadvantage, for nothing was more common among them, than to uſe their Deities upon the ſlighteſt occaſion. By *Jupiter*, by *Hercules*, &c. were almoſt continually in the Mouths of their Vertuous Characters. No Speech was ſpoke but was accompany'd by one of their Gods. This I hope no one will miſtake for an Authority for that abominable Sin; it is only to ſhow Mr. *Collier*, his Cauſe is here entirely loſt. And ſo I ſhall proceed to the next thing he Charges our Poets with, *viz.* their uſing Scripture Phraſes in their Plays.

And how they can avoid it I know not, unleſs this Critical Gentleman will make a New Language, and a New Alphabet for them; if he will promiſe to do this, I will engage in the Name of all the Poets, that there ſhall not be any Scripture Expreſſion us'd in Poetry. And to ſhow, that this is not ſo heinous as Mr. *Collier* Repreſents it; I ſhall offer theſe Conſiderations.

Firſt, That the Tranſlation of the *Holy Bible* being done ſo lately, there are contained in it the Phraſes and Idiom now in preſent uſe.

Secondly, The Sacred Scripture having ſuch excellent variety of Matter, and being ſo admirably adapted to all Eſtates and Conditions of Life, it contains all the different Phraſes that can be met with in the *Engliſh* Tongue.

This

This being ſo, I can ſcarce find it poſſible for a Poet to avoid the ſame manner of Expreſſion with the Tranſlators of the Holy Scriptures. Mr. *Collier* may as well forbid all of his Order to Preach, becauſe they muſt of neceſſity make uſe of ſome Phraſes, that have been us'd before to an ill purpoſe. To make this plainer I will only deſire Mr. *Collier* to compare thoſe places of their Plays which he quotes, with the Text of a *Bible* of an old Tranſlation, and he will find a very wide difference both in Words and Senſe. I ſuppoſe he will not deny the old Tranſlation to be Scripture. Beſides, how can he be poſitive he hits the true meaning of the Poet? Words may be wreſted to a quite contrary Senſe of their Author, and that made to appear ill in a Quotation, which is not ſo of it ſelf. How can he be ſure that Mr. *Congreve* intended to ridicule Religion, when he made *Valentine* in his Madneſs ſay *he was Truth?* 'Tis very probable Mr. *Congreve* intended no ſuch matter; and if he did not, Mr. *Collier* is guilty of Falſhood and Slander. The Heathen *Epictetus* can teach him more Charity, if the Bible cannot; he will tell him *That there are two handles for every thing, and that we ought to take hold of the beſt*; we ſhould always Judge favourably, and not put the worſt Conſtruction on things that they'l bear. But Mr. *Collier* is ſo much us'd to Private and Shrewd Meanings himſelf, that he imagines ſo of every one elſe, his very finding fault with others, betrays ſomething of guilt in himſelf; and becauſe he ſhall not complain that he is ill and uncharitably dealt with in this Cenſure, I ſhall give one Inſtance from many, to make good my Aſſertion. It is in the firſt Vol. of his *Eſſays*, Page 120. in his Chap. of the Aſpect. There he ſays, *Whether the Honeſty and Diſhoneſty are diſcernable in the Face, is a Queſtion which admits of Diſpute. King* Charles

the

the Second thought he could depend upon these Observations: But, with submission, I believe an instance might be given, in which his Rules of Phisiognomy fail'd. Now I fancy Mr. *Collier* had some shrewd meaning in this particular Instance, and I think he cannot complain of hard usage, if we believe we find this meaning in the 295th Page of Sir *William Temple*'s *Memoires*: For considering the Man and his Principles, it is more than probable our Supposition is right. And I think this is a meaning which he deserves to be call'd to Account for; those of his Party think it is sufficient if they express themselves obscurely enough to escape the lash of the Law; and have the impudence to write the most Scandalous Libels on their Superiors, under the shelter of a Double Meaning; it wou'd be but just if their Obscurities and Double Meanings were narrowly inpected, and themselves made to smart for the Liberty they have taken. Mr. *Collier* may make a great Bustle, and say this is hard usage; but let him learn better Manners for the future.

Further, supposing our Plays may have that Prophaness in them which he pretends, yet let him remember that Plays are the Glasses of Human Actions, and reflect the true Images of the People; as you see the Errors of your Complexion by a view in a Glass, so in the Play-House you see the meanness and folly of your Vices, and by beholding the frightful Image, you grow asham'd, and perhaps may Reform, whereas had they never been expos'd, they had still been your Darling Companions, tho' all the Pulpits in Town had thunder'd never so loudly against them. For as the Divine *Herbert* says,

> *A Verse may find him who a Sermon flies,*
> *And turn Delight into a Sacrifice.*

But

But now he proceeds to show how the Ancients us'd their Religion, and here he is forc'd to confess, against his will, That they almost equal'd the Moderns; but I say positively, they surpass'd us here too; and out-did, whatever he, with all his straining can pretend to alledge against our Poets. *Aristophanes* he has himself mark'd for a down-right Atheist, one, that brought the Deities to be publickly Ridicul'd upon the Stage; Nor do we find they had much better Treatment in their most solemn Tragedies. In several places of *Æschylus*, they, and Religion too, are far from being decently Treated. Nay, *Euripides*, who is the most Grave and Moral of all the Ancients both *Greeks* and *Latins*, was once Condemned, and had like to have Suffered Death for his Irreverent and Irreligious Treatment of the Gods. And *Sophocles*, who is called the Prince of Tragick Poets, makes often times mad work with the Deities: You see them scuffle and fall together by the Ears like a Rabble or a confus'd Multitude, upon none, or very ridiculous occasins. Nor is *Homer* himself in his *Epick Poem* free from these Indecencies, witness the Dissentions and Tumults of the Deities; some siding with the *Greeks*, others with the *Trojans*, and each hurrying about in the Service of the Party they had Espous'd. Among the *Latins*, the Neat and Correct *Terence* has given several Bold, and Exceptionable strokes about Religion: and I am very sure he will not be able to defend *Plautus* from the Objection, who often uses the Gods very coursly, witness the Prologue to *Amphitryon*, where he makes *Mercury* talk in Puns and Quibbles to the Audience, and the same Comical Character he wears throughout the Play. *Jupiter* himself is Represented Lewd and an Adulterer; *Arcturus* another of the Deities speaks the Prologue to his *Rudens*, and

and *Neptune*, one of their Principal Gods, suffers many a hard Banter in the Play. *Seneca* in his Tragedies often falls foul on the Gods, Providence, and Religion. I think the very worst he can pretend of our Modern Poets, is nothing compar'd with the Boldness the Ancients have taken on this Head. Nor is it a sufficient Excuse to say they were Heathens, and therefore cannot be suppos'd to be so strict as Christians ought to be; nor that *it is no wonder to find them run Riot upon this Subject*; for these were the Gods they pray'd to in their Adversity, and from whom they expected Relief and Help; they Confided in them, and Consecrated Temples to their Honour, Sung Hymns in Praise of their Goodness, and dreaded their Wrath: So that of Consequence they might have expected better usage from their Adorers. But I shall proceed to what he says of the Clergy.

And here he is very Copious indeed, and spends abundance of pains, to show what Venerable Thoughts the Ancients had of their Priests; and I think to very little purpose, for I believe the People of *England* (not excepting the Poets) have as high a Veneration for the Sacred Order as any Nation in the World have, or ever had: Let us observe a little how they are respected in other Countries.

In *France* we shall find them just as much Slaves to the Despotick Wills of their Princes, as the meanest Peasant of their Dominions; they must square their Doctrine to the Relish and Palate of the Court, or they are sure to smart for their Neglect. In *Holland* we find their Preachers are paid their Salaries by the State, which practise I suppose was founded upon the Observation of the many Disorders, and Tumults, have been rais'd and fomented in other Countries by the Ambition, or some other Passion of Priests. In *Italy* and *Spain* we find the Clergy living at their Ease, in the midst of Pomp and Riches, and very often taking as deep draughts of Luxury and Worldly Vanities, as the grossest Instance of Heathen Lewdness can afford. And tho' they pretend to exact an implicit Faith from the ignorant Laity, yet all that have been in those Countries assure us, That their Priests are look'd upon but as Hypocrites and Scandalous Persons; nor will the meanest Person stick at vilifying and ridiculing the Clergy, when they can do it safely. How often have we seen the Pope's Bulls and Orders tore and despis'd by Princes of their own Communion? And his Legates Imprison'd or Expell'd their Dominions. I speak not this to encourage any Contempt of the Sacred Order, for it ought, I think, to be treated with all imaginable Respect and Reverence, especially by us here in *England*, who are blest with the Soberest, and Gravest, as well as the most Learned Clergy of the whole World. We very rarely, if ever, meet with those Enormities and Disorders among the Clergy of *England*, which are so frequently seen amongst those of Foreign Countries. And here I cannot but by the way observe, That the Tumults and Civil War in *Poland* have no other source but the Ambition and Obstinate Humour of a Priest. And the Blood of some Hundreds of Innocent People have been Sacrificed to his Pride and Willfulness. now this very Instance being so full in the Eye of the whole World, it is no wonder if some Considering Observers exclaim, and lash out into Satyr upon the Occasion. Who can forbear? Nay, Mr. *Collier* himself, and all others of his Principles, are more bitter and sharp Invectives against the Order, by their Refractory and Obstinate Separation from the Greatest and most Pious Part of their Brethren, than any can be writ by the most

moſt Atheiſtical Pen; and wound it more ſeverely. To let this paſs. Mr. *Collier* himſelf owns *Oedipus* in *Sophocles*, to Reproach and Reflect on *Tireſias* the Prieſt, but to extenuate the matter, ſays, it is only on his Perſon, not his Function, thoſe ſharp ſtrokes are beſtow'd; and pray what do the *Engliſh* Poets do more? All their Reflections are, I really believe, intended for no other Deſign, but to hurt thoſe that deſerve them: The Satyr therefore is Innocent, and thoſe may thank themſelves it hits. The great ſtir Mr. *Collier* makes on this Head, gives great cauſe to ſuſpect, he is more than ordinarily concern'd in the Matter. *The more Clamour, the more Guilt*, has always prov'd a true Obſervation. He keeps a wondrous buſtle by a Quotation from *Tully*, and Obſervations from ſeveral Nations,to prove the Clergy as fit to be at the Head of Temporal as Spiritual Affairs; but here I think he is beſide his Byas; if we conſider the wide difference there is between them, we need go no farther to confute the Ambitious Gentleman. Mr. *Collier* hopes *what he has offered on this Head will not be miſunderſtood*; he aſſures us *there is no Vanity in the Caſe*. No ſquinting towards himſelf in the Matter. Now I can't ſuppoſe there is, how ſhou'd, what is ſpoke of the Clergy, any way relate to a Spruce Gentleman, a *Beau* with a Long Wig, Silk Waſtcoat, and Sword by his Side. For my part I think they are two very different Perſons. We will now examin his next Charge, which is their Immorality, their making *Debauchees* their top Characters and Rewarding them in the end

And upon this Head, this Critical Gentleman is very ſevere, tho' if Delight be the chief end of Comedy, as I think no one need to queſtion, the buſineſs will be found to bear much harder upon thoſe of his own Order than upon the Poets: For, the Poet's business being to please his Audience, he must Study their Humours and Fancies, and not his own; for, tho' the *Dramma* be never so regularly writ, yet every thing Represented, will seem Nauseous and Insipid, unless it is Conformable to the Sentiments and Relish of the Spectators. Whatever Poet follows not this Rule exactly, will quickly be sensible of his Error, by his bad Harvest of Fame and Profit. And if the Audience will not be pleas'd with any thing but Immorality, &c. pray why have not the Clergy, whose business it is to Instruct the People, taught them better? Which if they had, they wou'd have found the Poets to have follow'd the steps of their Audience. So that we see it is rather the Clergy's Fault than the Poet's Crime, that our *Drammas* are Irregular on this Head. And Mr. *Collier* has laid his Argument just wrong, for if the World be good, Plays wou'd be good also; but if the World be bad, Plays will be bad too: And I am sure the Ancients were fully as Guilty, if not more Criminal on this Account. In *Sophocles* and *Aristophanes*, we may find several Instances of Vice Rewarded and Escaping Unpunished. In almost every Play of *Terence* we may see Vice Rewarded: *Chærea* is made happy in the *Eunuch* after having Debauch'd a Virgin, and he generlly does the same in all his Plays; nay, you will not only see Profligate Lewd Sparks enjoy their their Mistresses, but the Common Courtezans themselves Rewarded and Honoured. *Plautus* will afford several Examples to our purpose, However, granting we do sometimes see on our Theatres Instances of Vice Rewarded, or at least unpunish'd, yet it ought not to be an Argument against the Art, any more than the Extravagancies and Ill Practises of *some in Orders* can be against the whole Body of the Clergy. And here

I

I cannot but call to mind a Sentence I have somewhere met with, *That much of ill Nature, and a very little Judgment, go far in finding the faults of others.* How nearly this may affect Mr. *Collier* I leave himself to consider: But I shall say no more on this Head; nor shall I follow him in his Reflections on *Amphytrion*, *Don Quixot*, and the *Relapse*, but leave him to the handling of the Gentleman who are more nearly concern'd. I shall consider his Quotations from the Fathers, which he Levels against all manner of Stage-Plays. I thought the Learned Mr. *Collier* cou'd not have been so mistaken in the Matter, for let him consider that these Fathers liv'd in Heathen Times, and several of them under *Pagan Princes*, by whom Idolatry, and all manner of Vice, was not only tolerated, but openly Encourag'd on the Stage. We need not wonder at the bitter Invectives we find dispers'd in their Writings against those Devilish Representations: the wicked Shows of their Gladiators, and Women often times fighting Naked in their Theatres, were a just Cause for the Indignation of those Zealous and Good Men; and deserv'd their severest Reproof. But all those Wickednesses are Banish'd our Stage, so that I cannot see how Mr. *Collier* cou'd apply them to his purpose, but they might serve his Vanity tho' not his Cause, the World was to be acquainted with his Familiarity with the Learned Ancients, and some Credit might be gain'd by the Company he kept, But it may happen contrary to his Expectations, his Mistake in the Mattter may go near to frustrate his Hopes. For when the Matter requires Testimonies against Tragedies and Comedies, he presently brings in places of Fathers against the Spectacles of Fencing, Bear-Baiting, Horse-Racing, and such other Games, no more like Stage Plays, than a Huffing Gentleman is like an Humble, Meek Clergy-Man; or Malice

lice and ill Nature, like Wit and Learning. And for once I ſhall ſhow this Critical Gentleman a Miſtake he will not be able to defend. In his 250th Page he tranſlates *Spectacula Secularia*, Stage-Plays; I thought Mr. *Collier* better underſtood the *Roman Hiſtory*, than to miſtake Shews that were to be acted but once in a Hundred Years for Stage-Plays, but it is his Miſtake through all his Quotations. He gives us a very large one from *Tertullian*, but let us obſerve the Circumſtance of the Matter, and we ſhall find it will do him no good at all; for *Tertullian* lived in the Time of *Septimius Severus*, Emperor of *Rome*, under whom was rais'd a Cruel Perſecution againſt the Chriſtians; in the Twelfth Year of his Reign were Proclaim'd the Secular *Plays*, (ſo called, becauſe they were Solemnis'd but *Semel in Sæculo*, once in a Hundred Years) which Mr. *Collier* very learnedly miſtakes for Stage-Plays; they were Dedicated to the Honour of ſeveral of their Heathen Gods: *Tertullian* conceiving it might breed great Scandal to the Chriſtian Religion, if Chriſtians ſhou'd Reſort to them, Writes a Treatiſe, Exhorting all Chriſtians to forbear theſe Shews, and uſes many Excellent and Weighty Reaſons to ſhew that theſe *Plays* were full of Idolatry and Superſtition, and therefore they cou'd not go to ſee them, but they muſt become as Acceſſaries and Partners with them in their Wickedneſs; That they were full of Licentious Beaſtlineſs; That Men and Women were brought in Naked upon the Publick Stage, uſing many Laſcivious and Obſcene Poſtures; That themſelves were under Perſecution, and fitter to *Mourn* than to be *Merry*; That their Afflictions called rather for Tears and Grief, than Joy and Laughter. Now what Divine among us wou'd not have Writ juſt as *Tertullian* did upon that Occaſion? But how Mr.

Mr. *Collier* can ſtrain this againſt our *Stage-Plays*, I cannot imagine; Is there the leaſt Similitude betwixt them? But this Gentleman obſerves no Circumſtances, if he can but rake Words enough he is ſatisfy'd, not minding if they are pertinent to his purpoſe. Mr. *Collier* reckons *Plays* among the *Pomps* and *Vanities* we have Vow'd againſt in our Baptiſm, but *Tertullian* ſays poſſitively, *If there be no Idol in the Play, and Idolatry be not committed in it, then I charge it not with any renouncing which we made in Baptiſm.* And that it was none: But Heathen *Plays* the Fathers meant, we may find by the Words of St. *Cyprian*, *Quod Spectatulum ſine Idolo? Quis Ludus ſine Sacrificio?* All his Decrees of Council will be taken from him by the ſame Reaſon, for they were only meant of the Idolatrous Heathen Shews; the Decree that he Inſtances in, of the 3d Council of *Carthage*, plainly proves it, by mentioning particularly the *Spectacula Secularia*, the *Sæcular Games*, and calling them *Pagan* Entertainments: His Quotations from Heathen Authors will not fare better than their Companions, for they cannot be imagin'd to relate to any thing but their own Heathen Shews. However, we will ſee preſently if we have none of their Authorities on our ſide. But firſt I will aſſert that our Modern Poets, and eſpecially the *Engliſh*, have excell'd all the Ancients in Theatrical Performances, They have caſt off that unneceſſary Clog the *Chorus*, which is manifeſtly for the better, thereby freeing their *Drammas* from many groſs Abſurdities. Our Moderns are not Guilty of ſpeaking and Addreſſing themſelves to the Audience in the midſt of the Action, which is apt to cauſe ſuch Confuſion in the Spectators, that they cannot judge what belongs to the Play, and what does not; the Ancients were very frequently guilty of this fault. Their Plots were for the moſt part

ſingle,

ſingle, without any Turns or admirable Surpriſes to delight or refreſh the Audience; their Characters had no Variety of Humour, with which our *Engliſh* Stage ſo excellently abounds; when you ſee one or two of their Plays, you ſee all the different Humours of their Theatres, you are ſure to meet with the ſame Covetous Old Man, the ſame Lewd Young Spark, the ſame Debauch'd Courtezan, and the ſame Saucy Slave in all their Comedies. Now how this ſhou'd conſtantly Delight, I know not; I am very ſure it wou'd quickly be hiſs'd with us; beſide, it ſhews a very Narrow Converſation, or Obſervation, (for upon that Humour depends) in their Poets; and plainly proves a Fancy very Barren. With us you are differently Delighted every Day, you meet with Variety, you find ſomething always New on our Theatres. This one thing alone will carry us far beyond any of the Ancients; and Mr. *Collier* himſelf muſt own, when any of our Poets have Choſe the Subjects of the Ancients, that they have far ſurpaſſed them; better Modell'd the Plot, and contriv'd the Incidents more ſurpriſing and admirable, nay and more probable too, have work'd their Thoughts to a greater Elegancy, and made the Turns more Nice, Eaſie, and Sublime, and their Characters, which were often Irregular, more Juſt, and Natural. We may eaſily prove what is here aſſerted, by only comparing our *Oedipus* with *Sophocles* among the *Greeks*, or our *Amphytrion* with *Plautus* among the *Latins*. If we have any regard to that Ornament to Learning, and Glory to his Country, Sir *William Temple*, we need argue the matter no farther; for Diſcourſing of *Drammatick Poetry* in his *Miſſelanea* 2d. Part, he poſitively gives the Preference to the Moderns, denying that the Ancients can ſo much as ſtand in Competition with them.

I ſhall now endeavour at ſome Defence of Plays; and for this, I think I need not put my ſelf to much trouble; for if we conſider its Antiquity, its Uſefulneſs, and the general Eſteem and Encouragement it has met with in all Civiliz'd and Polite Nations, we cannot but agree in very Noble Thoughts of it. Firſt of its Antiquity.

And here I might Trace its Original from *Theſpis*, and ſhew its ſeveral Gradual Improvements by *Æſchylus*, *Euripides*, and *Sophocles*, and from thence follow it to the *Romans*, who muſt own the *Greeks* to have been their Maſters in this Species of Poetry; *Terence*'s Comedies are hardly any more but bare Tranſlations of *Menander*; and *Plautus* ſtands very much indebted to *Ariſtophanes*. But I ſhall wave this Head as foreign to my purpoſe, and not fit for the ſcanty limits of a Letter, which is grown too long already, and ſhall proceed to its Uſefulneſs.

Which is ſo manifeſt, that I wonder any one can queſtion it, who conſiders how well adapted it is to the Intentions of Human Life, Profit, and Delight. Who can expreſs the Charms of a well wrought Scene lively Repreſented? The Motions of the Actor Charm our outward Senſes, while the pleaſing Words ſteals into our Souls, and mixes with our very Blood and Spirits, ſo that we are carry'd by an irreſiſtleſs, but pleaſing violence into the very Paſſion we behold. What Heart can forbear relenting to ſee an unfortunate Perſon, for ſome unhappy miſtakes in his Conduct, fall into irreparable Misfortunes? This ſtrikes deep into our Breaſts, by a tender inſinuation ſteals into our Souls, and draws a Pity from us; ſo conſequently making us ready to aſſiſt all that we meet with in a like Condition: it teaches us to Judge Charitably of the Miserable, when we see a small Error ignorantly committed, may be the cause of heavy Misfortunes; it teaches us at the same time Caution, and Circumspection in the Management of our selves. And who that sees a Vitous Person severely Punish'd, will not tremble at Vice? I think the *Libertine Destroy'd* cannot fail to put serious Thoughts into the most hardened and profligate Atheist, and rouze him from his Diabolical Lethargy, as powerfully as the loudest Denunciations from the Pulpit. Nor is Comedy without its Excellencies, which being a lower and more natural Representation than Tragedy, discovers to us the daily Affairs we meet with in the World; and if Tragedy scares us out of our Vices, Comedy will no less shame us out of our Follies. Tragedy, like a severe Master, keeps a heavy hand over us; but Comedy, like an indulgent Parent, mixes something to please when it reproves. Who can forbear blushing, that sees some Darling Folly expos'd? And tho' its ridiculousness tickles him into a laughter, yet at the same time he feels a secret shame for the Guilt. *Aristophanes* kept all the *Athenians* in Awe by his Satyr; a Person was no sooner guilty of a Crime in the City, but it star'd him full in the Face on the Stage, and by this means he regulated the Commonwealth better than their greatest Philosopers with their empty Sophisms, or the Laws with their blunted edge. Comedy is also useful to instruct us in in our Dealings in the World; when we see a Friend False and Treacherous, this teaches us to stand upon our Guard, and be very cautious whom we trust; when we see a Young Gentleman Ruin'd by the Subtile and Deluding Arts of some Cunning Courtezan, it bids us beware of the like Danger: The *Squire* of *Alsatia* gives more effectual Instructions to the Country Gentleman, for the avoiding his Ruin both in Person and Estate by the Town-Sharpers, by exposing their Shifts and Cheats, that the best Advice of the

ablest

ableſt Divines, Thus ſeeing of what Worth and Value *Dramatick Poetry* is, for the forming our Manners and regulating our Lifes, beſides the great Delight and Pleaſure it affords us: I think I need not urge much more for its Recommendation.

If we look back to *Athens*, we ſhall find that that Learned Commonwealth took the greateſt Care of their Theatres, and that they ſpent more Coſt in Adorning and Decorating them, than they did in all their Wars. *Euripides*, and *Sophocles*, were reckoned Equal, if not Superior to their Greateſt Philoſophers: Their Actors were generally Perſons of Good Birth and Education; nay, ſometimes we find Kings themſelves performing on their Theatres, and *Cornelius Nepos* in *Præfat. Vit.* aſſures us, That to appear on the Publick Stage, was not in the leaſt Injurious to any Man's Character or Honour. The *Romans*, tho' they did not reſpect their Stage equal with the *Greeks*, yet had their *Ædiles*, Magiſtrates Choſe on purpoſe to Reward their Deſerving Actors, and take Care of the Theatres. *Macrobius* tells us in his ſeventh Chapter, how *Auguſtus Cæſar* himſelf Rewarded *Liberius*, and *Publius*, *Pylades*, and *Hylas*, four Players in *Rome*. The Famous *Brutus* was not only a great Favourer of *Plays* himſelf, but he writ to *Cicero* that he ſhou'd frequent the Theatres. And *Pompey* the Great built a Theatre at his own Coſt and Charge. *Suetonius Tranquillus* tells us of the very beſt of all the *Roman* Emperors, *Auguſtus Cæſar*, That, *Spectaculorum, & aſſiduitate, & varietate, & Magnificentia, omnes Anteceſſit.* In the Variety and Magnificence, and frequenting of *Plays*, he exceeded all Men. And the Famous *Cicero* ſays, *Et noſmetipſi, qui ab delectatione omni negotiis impedimur; & in ipsa Occupatione delectationes alias multas habere possumus, ludis tamen Oblectamur, & ducimur.* And in another place speaking of *Plays*, he says, *Delectant homines, mihi crede, ludi, non eos solum, qui fatentur, sed illos etiam qui dissimulant:* All People, believe me, are pleas'd and delighted with *Plays*, not only those that confess it, but those that dissemble and wou'd deny it; nay, then the Learned *Cicero* must be a Lyar, or good Mr. *Collier* a Hypocrite. It is moreover observable from the History of all Ages, that the Theatres are (if I may use the Expression) the Pulse of a Kingdom; by the Low or Flourishing Condition of the Former, you are certain of the Estate of the Latter, when the One is at its Height, the Other is at its full Glory; and when the One is Mean and Despicable, the Other is sure to be Poor and Low. And indeed I admire any one can have a Thought toward the Discouragement of any sort of *Poetry*, who considers how highly *Poets* were priz'd and esteem'd by the Ancients; the Great Emperour *Augustus* thought himself more happy in the Private Conversation of his *Virgil* and *Horace*, than when Deck'd with all his Royalty, and Seated on his Throne. The Fam'd *Scipio* and the Noble *Lælius* were proud when they Enjoy'd their *Terence*. And the Celebrated *Cicero* has thus spoke in their Praise. *Atqui sic a summis hominibus Eruditissimisq; accepimus cæterarum rerum studia, & Doctrina, et Præceptis, et Arte constare; Poetam Natura ipsa Valere, et mentis viribus excitari, et quasi Divino quodam spiritu Afflari; quare suo Jure noster Ennius Sanctos appellat Poetas, quod quasi Deorum aliquo dono, et Munere commendati esse Videantur.* But it is time, to hasten to an end, I shall add but one saying more, from the Learned Sir *William Temple*'s *Miscellanea* 2d Part, where speaking

ſpeaking of *Poetry*, he tells us, *He that is inſenſible of its Charms, ſhou'd take care to hide it, that it is not known; for fear he bring in queſtion his Good Nature, if not his Underſtanding.* And ſo I ſhall conclude with Subſcribing my ſelf,

SIR,

Your very Humble

Servant, &c.